DEFINING
POLITICAL
DEVELOPMENT

New Books in the Series

- Exploring the Stability of Deterrence
  edited by Jacek Kugler and Frank C. Zagare

- Arms Transfers to the Third World: Probability Models of
  Superpower Decisionmaking   *Gregory S. Sanjian*

- Nigeria and the International Capitalist System
  edited by Toyin Falola and Julius Ihonvbere

- Defining Political Development
  Stephen Chilton

DEFINING POLITICAL DEVELOPMENT

Stephen Chilton

GSIS Monograph Series
in World Affairs

THE UNIVERSITY OF DENVER

Lynne Rienner Publishers • Boulder & London

Published in the United States of America in 1988 by
Lynne Rienner Publishers, Inc.
948 North Street, Boulder, Colorado 80302

and in the United Kingdom by
Lynne Rienner Publishers, Inc.
3 Henrietta Street, Covent Garden, London WC2E 8LU

Chilton, Stephen.
    Defining political development / by Stephen Chilton.
        p.   cm. — (GSIS monograph series in world affairs)
    Bibliography: p.
    Includes index.
    ISBN 1-55587-086-4
    1. Political psychology.   2. Political culture.   I. Title.
II. Series.
JA74.5.C527 1988
306'.2—dc19   87-19416
                                                    CIP

Printed and bound in the United States of America

The paper used in this publication meets the
requirements of the American National Standard
for Permanence of Paper for Printed Library
Materials Z39.48-1984. ⊗

Contents

List of Tables and Figure   vi

Acknowledgments   vii

1   Five Fundamental Theoretical Challenges in   1
Conceptualizing Political Development

2   The Locus of Development, the Micro-Macro   23
Connection, and Exact Specification

3   Normative Justification   37

4   The Hierarchy of Forms of Political Culture   67

5   Developmental Dynamics   79

6   Theoretical Implications   101

Bibliography   113

Index   125

About the Book and the Author   135

Tables and Figure

Table 1   Four Levels of Theorization in Three Fields   15

Table 2   Speculative Classification of Cultural Stages   43

Table 3   Speculative Classification of Social Forms   68

Figure 1   The "Steady-State Society"   32

Acknowledgments

Fifteen years of any project generate more debts than can be repaid short of writing another book. Nevertheless, I must thank Professors Roy Feldman, Frederick W. Frey, Everett Hagen, the late Lawrence Kohlberg, and Lucian Pye for inspiring and educating this stubborn ex-mathematician. I also thank my parents and Professors Karen Feste, Beth Lau, and Steve Ropp for their support during a long and difficult labor. Professors Bill Eamon and Steve Seidman provided valuable information and incredulity. Professor Zagorka Golubovic provided intelligent criticism of my reading of Marx. Professors Craig Grau and Guntram Werther gave this work the benefit of their close, intelligent scrutiny. I deeply appreciate the professional assistance of Lynne Rienner and her friendly, professional staff. Of course, the weaknesses and errors remain my responsibility.

ONE

Five Fundamental Theoretical Challenges in Conceptualizing Political Development

The central role of political development in the debates over Vietnam in the late 1960s led me to question the definition of development. It seemed that our society needed, but apparently had not been able to find, a normatively grounded, practically useful, analytic framework for the study and practice of political development. Applying the theoretical approaches of political development, political psychology, and political power analysis to the Vietnam war gradually led me to focus on certain abstract, theoretical problems as central to the debate over political development: fundamental conceptual challenges that, even if difficult to meet, were nevertheless guides to the heart of the issue.

The first of these problems was how to ground a theory of development normatively. U.S. justifications of its Vietnam policy explicitly relied on the normative claims of democracy. Opponents of the war derided those claims as false, as a blind, or as ethnocentric, but, even while opposing the war myself, I felt that reliance on normative arguments was at least apposite. Public policy had to rely on *some* normative vision; the problem was to find solid moral ground.

The second problem was to assess the relative importance and interconnections of institutional and individual change in political development. This challenge was raised by the status of democracy in Vietnam. U.S. attempts to create the outward forms and rituals of democracy had not affected the "hearts and minds" of the Vietnamese people, and it became increasingly apparent that they simply practiced their political business as

1

usual while preserving a democratic facade for foreign consumption. Cultural relativists of the time claimed that democracy was not relevant to the Vietnamese culture, but that seemed too easy an answer. Doctrinaire cultural relativism represents an abandonment of our common humanity, not to mention an abandonment of meaningful research into cultural variation, and I was reluctant to accept such an answer. In addition, democratic principles simply did not seem ethnocentric to me: a feeble reason when spoken by a Westerner, I suppose, but there it was. Finally, I had become aware, from Lucian Pye's (1966b) essay "Democracy and Political Development," that democracy required not just institutions and rituals but also particular citizen competencies. Pye also insisted that individual behavior, not just institutional form, was important. What I had encountered was, of course, the challenge of making the micro-macro connection: to create a theory of development in which individual change and institutional change appear as coordinate elements.

Later, I discovered Lawrence Kohlberg's Piagetian theory of moral reasoning and realized that in this developmental approach lay the answer to the problem of normative grounding: in its concentration on reasoning, on cognitive structure, and on cognitive ambiguity as the source of development. These virtues were not dependent on Kohlberg's specific empirical methods. I took for granted the general validity of his research, though I am grateful for his creation of an accurate scoring instrument.

Kohlberg's theory concerned individuals, however, and the micro-macro connection was not yet made. I eventually ran across symbolic interactionism and Talcott Parsons's trichotomy of systems, and wove them into my concept of political culture. All that remained was to clarify, to explain, and to spin out the implications of the resulting logical structure. Among those implications were the answers to the remaining theoretical challenges I had seen as necessary for any adequate definition of the concept. In addition, general knowledge about genetic epistemology and the exercise of social power in symbolic systems provided a good deal of "near-empirical" information about how change actually comes to occur.

The result is an analytic work that addresses two theoretical questions: "What is political development?" and "How should we approach its study?" It seeks to relate the central elements of political development in a way that guides specific theories toward answers which, taken together, address the five fundamental theoretical challenges in conceptualizing political development. The concepts of individual, cultural, and social system; the role played by reasoning, and especially moral reasoning, in maintaining institutions; the concept of cognitive ambiguity and its consequences for cognitive development; and the concepts of public commonness and of hegemonic control over its production—these are the central elements of the analytic framework.

The work presents neither a theory of political development nor an empirical analysis of developing societies. It does not (in any immediate way) provide answers to specific questions like: "What is the role of the military in development?" or "What are the prospects for the political development of the Seychelles?" It is not an empirical work at all except insofar as it illuminates and reinforces old results by drawing them together in its theoretical framework.

It is important to note that in this work the "political" in "political development" broadly denotes any way in which people relate to one another: through governmental institutions, the traditional meaning of politics (e.g., bureaucracies and other regimes); through economic institutions (such as the open market); or through social institutions (such as the nuclear family or specific religions). These areas of study are deliberately not distinguished here, because a reconstruction of development theory must begin with only those distinctions necessary to it. As Bloch (1961:59) argues: "For though the artificial conception of man's activities which prompts us to carve up the creature of flesh and blood into the phantoms *homo oeconomicus, philosophicus, juridicus* is doubtless necessary, it is tolerable only if we refuse to be deceived by it." (Compare Lukács, 1971.) The academic, disciplinary distinctions among these areas of society may eventually be found to stem from true differences in their objects of study; but even if so, these true differences must emerge only as necessary consequences of the analysis. One of the intellectual tragedies of the last century was the separation of "political economy" into "political science" and "economics." The forms of analysis thereafter possible were greatly restricted, and the capacity of either discipline for critical analysis was severely weakened. To predicate this essay on unnecessary intellectual divisions could permit an equally fatal result. In this work, then, the terms political development,

development, economic development, and social development are synonymous, even though as a political scientist I tend to use political development most often.

Political Development

Political development is important to social science because it poses hard theoretical problems. Any discussion of development implicitly presupposes answers to two fundamental theoretical challenges: making the micro-macro connection between individuals and institutions in development; and providing normative justification of the sequence. These challenges are both extremely difficult to solve and extremely important: Elder and Cobb (1983:144-145) term the micro-macro problem one of "the most basic and perennial questions in political analysis," and, as will be seen later, the difficulty of providing normative justification for the concept of development has led at least two analysts to recommend abandoning it. Development thus serves as a laboratory for social theorists, and social theorists as diverse as Marx, Parsons, Weber, and Durkheim have all worked there.

Political development is also important as a guide to the origins of social institutions, and thereby to a better understanding of those institutions' current meaning. To paraphrase Piaget's (1970:4) statement about scientific knowledge, we cannot say that on the one hand there is the history of political institutions, and on the other political institutions as they are today; there is simply a continual transformation and reorganization. This fact implies that knowledge of the historical and psychological origins of these changes helps us understand the nature of the resulting institutions.

Political development is also important for practical reasons. Our theoretical concern with the origins of institutions parallels our practical concerns: only in the reality of practical concerns can we validate our theoretical discoveries of the active principle of development.[1] Furthermore, our most important political issues involve political development. Though the term is rarely applied in domestic politics, questions about the proper relationship of the state and the economy are developmental in that they contemplate the restructuring of social institutions. In international politics, development affects what regimes will be in power, and for how long; what the relationships among countries will be; what policies toward us different countries will adopt; and thus, ultimately, what our policies toward them should be.

Despite its importance, the concept of political development has long been in a state of confusion. The term came to political science from a sense that there must be a political analogue to the widely used concept of economic development (Eckstein, 1982). Political science thus acquired a label for the concept and a sense of its potential significance, but not much else. Many "political development" works give little attention to conceptualization. For example, despite its title, the recent *Understanding Political Development* (Weiner and Huntington, 1987) contains no index entry for the term,[2] even though the work begins with an acknowledgment of the variety of definitions of political development (p. xiii). Richard Bensel's (1984) *Sectionalism and American Political Development 1880-1980* discusses political development only in the sense of "historical changes in the American political system," i.e., political developments. Other examples could be mentioned.[3] The resulting Tower of Babel in political development—innumerable, *ad hoc* definitions and theories—led Huntington (1971:304) to conclude that the concept should be abandoned. He argued that the concept neither integrated a body of related concepts nor distinguished one aspect of political reality from another.[4] Riggs (1981) goes even further by arguing that the term is not a concept but only a "power-word" that offers not analytical virtue but political power to those who can control it. Even Eckstein (1982:454), who seeks to refurbish the concept, admits that "the present literature on political development simply does not represent 'developmental' inquiry properly." Given this feeling even on the part of some of political development's best-known analysts, the concept appears to have fallen into disrepute or at least neglect.

Riggs's and Huntington's conclusions seem to be counsels of despair rather than measured responses to the problem. Riggs is certainly correct that political development is a power-word, but it does not follow that it is therefore incapable of definition. The term is a power-word because (as argued later) any conception of it must be normatively grounded. Definitions of development simultaneously assert a normative position. This normative aspect of the term has two consequences: (a) It gives political development its status as a power-word, since control over the definition is control over the social vision others must pursue; and (b) It creates its own difficulty of definition, since disputes over normative positions are notoriously numerous and hard to solve, and the covert nature of these disputes keeps them from being conducted rationally. Huntington is certainly correct when he notes the confusion of definitions, but it does not follow that the term should be abandoned.[5] Huntington's suggestion, "change," differs from "political development" in the former's absence of a normative position. Huntington might consider this absence an asset rather than a liability, but his "alternative" is illusory: a complete theory of change requires both a theory of normative judgments and, further, a normative position. In any event, the difficulties Huntington points out— the diversity of definitions and the scattered nature of the resulting research—do not require abandonment of "political development."

The question is, of course, how to define the term. Given the apparent importance of the concept and the widespread sense that it does exist, whatever the current diversity of its definitions, a more measured response would be to assess whether the concept might be defined in a way that overcomes the theoretical challenges from which our difficulties arise.[6]

The Locus of Development, Exact Specification, and the Micro-Macro Connection

Political development clearly arises from and affects individuals, cultural-institutional forms, and objective, regularized patterns of social interaction. This wide domain of interest raises three related problems: first, specifying what it is that develops; second, distinguishing political development from its constituents, correlates, causes, and consequences; and third, establishing what relationship exists in development between the individual and institutionalized behavior. These problems are here termed "the locus of development," "exact specification," and "the micro-macro connection," respectively.

To begin with, what is it that develops, exactly—individuals or cultural-institutional forms? We require a definition of political development that, while allowing for political development's operation in many areas, nonetheless locates it precisely as the development of some certain thing.[7] Are we seeking, with Hagen (1962), McClelland (1976), or Almond and Verba (1963), to locate development in an aggregation of innovators, achievers, or civic-minded actors whose advanced behavior constitutes development? Are we seeking, with Fitzgibbon (1956) or Smith (1969), to locate development in certain cultural-institutional forms whose structure constitutes development? Or, as Pye (1966a) argues, is political development a "syndrome," somehow embracing both individual and institutional behavior?

The choice of any of these basic approaches reveals further complexities. If we say that development is a matter of individual development, then what is it about individuals that develops? Their support for democratic norms? Their reasoning? Their empathy? Their need for achievement? Their sense of efficacy? If we say that development is a matter of institutional development, then what is it about institutions that develops? Their complexity? Their ascriptive norms? Their rationality? And in what institutions do we locate development? The institution of secret, free elections? Party competition? Freedom of the press? Representative democracy? Economic productivity? If we say that development is a syndrome, then what coherence does this syndrome have beyond the merely statistical correlation of its elements? Are all elements equally indicators of development?

Theorists have a natural impulse to finesse this problem through an eclectic approach. For example, Pye (1966a) lists a variety of definitions of political development, concluding that all are aspects of an underlying "development syndrome." Huntington (1987) notes the existence of many separate development goals. Such analyses have the virtue of pointing consciously to its many aspects, but they have the weakness of indiscriminately mixing development itself with its many associated aspects. These aspects may provide the raw material for useful operational definitions of development, but conceptualization must precede operationalization.

This raises the second of the challenges mentioned earlier—the problem of "exact specification." Political development must not be confused with its constituents, correlates, causes, or consequences. A precise concept must define development fully and must distinguish it from all related concepts.

Consider the confusion between political development and its constituents. If development researchers are interested in some constituent aspect (XYZ) of the development process, they say "political development is XYZ," thereby unconsciously implying that the concept is *solely* XYZ. For example, Huntington (1965:387) says that political development is "the institutionalization of political organizations and procedures," surely a somewhat limited vision of what political systems might become.[8] Karl Deutsch (1961:102) says that political development "is the process in which major clusters of old social, economic, and psychological concomitants are eroded or broken and people become available for new patterns of socialization and behavior." Again, this is surely an incomplete definition; a nuclear war would create a similar result without being considered a developmental process.

Researchers interested in the consequences of political development say "political development leads to XYZ," thus either leaving the concept undefined or, worse, implying that political development *is* XYZ. For example, David Apter (1968:2) defines political development as "a process which affects choice. The modernization focus helps to make sense of the choices likely to be at our disposal." But here Apter is speaking of a *consequence* of development (limitations on choice), surely not of development itself. Denis Goulet (1968:299) says that political development is "a crucial means of obtaining a good life." Even if true, this is not a definition of development.[9]

Researchers interested in causes or correlates may create corresponding definitional confusions.[10] Thus John Dorsey (1963:320) defines political development in terms of "the changes in power structure and processes that occur concomitantly with changes in energy conversion levels in the social system, whether such conversion levels change primarily in their political, social, and economic manifestations or in various combinations of the three." Such a formulation helps researchers identify when the process of political development is occurring, but it does not tell them what it is.[11]

The position that the conception of political development is fairly arbitrary, so that fine distinctions in its definition are of little analytical importance, is not correct. It might be valid if we were concerned only with naming phenomena, but there are three arguments against it. First, if the definition of political development is to allow us to study development's causes and consequences, development must be defined as distinct from them. Second, imprecise definitions of political development prevent seeing the total picture and throw off our analyses by misdirecting our attention to phenomena not properly part of development at all. In addition, if the development process has some coherence, then we will be able to understand it clearly only if we can examine all of it. Third, because the definition of political development must be normatively grounded—an issue to be raised shortly—we must take care in our definition to use only those elements whose normative implications we can support. For example, suppose "withdrawal of status respect" (Hagen, 1962) produces development. We would not want to define it carelessly as a constituent of development, because we would find ourselves defending withdrawal of status respect as a virtue in and of itself. Whatever the virtues of its consequences, withdrawal of status respect is clearly not a social condition one seeks for its own sake.

Political development cannot be defined solely in terms of either individual or institutional change. A concept of political development must show how both individuals and institutions change in the process of development. Institutional development clearly cannot take place without some associated change in individuals, nor can a theory of individual development without associated institutional change be regarded as political development. The easiest way to see this is to argue by contradiction—that is, by looking at how absurd consequences follow from defining development in terms of one of these aspects without the other. Consider, for example, the consequence of defining political development as a change in individuals alone. Such a position would require us to consider developed a society in which an overwhelming majority of highly developed (however defined) people were ruled in some brutal manner by a despotic, hereditary elite. The virtue of the people would not compensate for, or even much affect, the noxious effects of the brutal institutions.[12] Development is thus not solely a matter of individuals, even aggregated individuals.

Consider, on the other hand, the consequence of defining political development as a change in institutions alone. U.S. experience in Vietnam would lead us to reject this possibility. In Vietnam we attempted to impose our government's view of developed institutions on a people for whom they had no special meaning. The immediate subversion of the institutions resulted:

elections were rigged, local strongmen continued to hold sway, and for the most part Vietnamese business went on as usual behind the institutional facade. A similar tale is told about the original election of the Russian Duma: "Comprehension of party programmes and identities was extremely rudimentary. Villages sometimes made their choice collectively, or demanded instructions from the authorities to this effect. 'Why weren't we, dark and ignorant people, told for whom to vote?', ran one such complaint; and even in the towns a reaction of this kind was not unknown."[13] The virtue of institutions thus does not automatically and alone overcome contrary preferences of the people.

So if there is such a thing as development, then clearly it must consider both individuals and institutions and identify how the two are connected. (The unsupported assumption that one will follow from the other is inadequate.) An institution does not make individuals, nor do individuals (at least considered in isolation) make institutions. Although interdependent, they are in no sense identical to one another. Thus when one conceptualizes development, one must solve the problem of the micromacro connection: through what linkage does development result in both different individuals and different institutions?[14]

Specifying the Nature of Development

A concept of political development must include the possible states of development. As Payne (1984:35) puts it, "when we transfer the term [development from biology] to 'political development', the phrase is meaningless unless we supply the pictures [i.e., the states] the word 'development' requires as part of its operational definition." The "state of development" variable can take either continuous values, like GNP, or discontinuous values, like Maslow's need levels. This challenge requires only that its possible values be specified by the theorist.[15]

We should not press this requirement too far. In particular, we must not feel bound to specify levels of development beyond the highest level reached. It is entirely possible that, far from knowing what our developmental goal is, we construct our sense of development step by step, with each new vision built on its predecessor. Analogues of this exist in other fields. In Piaget's theory of cognitive development, the child constructs new cognitive stages in interaction with the environment, not from being taught the right way (the social learning model) or from "wired-in" physical changes (the maturation model). No "goal" exists, or to the extent one does, it is itself restructured in the developmental process. Again analogously, Marxian social theory believes itself to undergo successive refinement from interaction with the social world—the process of *praxis*. The assumption that we can foresee future development seems both ill-founded and theoretically unnecessary.

On the other hand, we should not fall into the opposing trap of believing that the highest level of development we have attained is the highest level possible. Theories of "modernity" seem particularly subject to this error in their implication that development is becoming "modern" and nothing further. (Adherents of such theories may not in fact maintain this implication, of course.) This mistake is disguised to some extent because "modernity" is a moving target. Without debating here the extent to which "modern" societies are in fact developed, we can at least agree not to assume that any current social arrangements are the terminus of development.[16]

Normative Grounding

Finally, a concept of political development must show that a "more developed" society is a better society. Development carries a normative connotation. This connotation is so strong that we use the very different term "change" to mean development absent normative implications. To discuss development rather than change requires some extra effort.

Why add to our burdens, however? Why should social scientists enter the morass of normative argumentation when, as Huntington (1971) points out, the study of "change" offers a firm, alternative path to the same issues? Furthermore, given the current disagreements over the very definition of development, how can its use be of any scientific value? And the problem is not merely that social scientists disagree over what development is, but, more to the point, that the supposed subjects of this concept—Third World societies—differ among themselves over the term's meaning. Even if social scientists were able to agree on what development means, what possible consequence would our agreement have for the real world? Would we not be guilty of the "idealistic fallacy" in assuming that our ideas and ideals have real consequences not just for us but also, ethnocentrically, for completely different cultures?[17] These questions thus raise two basic issues: whether normative questions have any significance in the material world and thus add anything to the study of change; and whether our particular normative conceptions will be significant to others.

First, the alternative of a nonnormative study of change is illusory. People choose how they wish to relate to one another, at least in part and at certain times, according to what they believe is right. Certainly there are impersonal forces in the world that act upon us (e.g., gravity), but social forces come from people, who may act in response to their ethical perspectives. People explain their own behavior by reference to what they felt was right given the situation. Political leaders justify their actions through explicitly ideological argument. People believe that moral reasons can and often do govern their behavior. We need not assume that ideas (e.g., a conception of what development is) are all-powerful to admit that they can make a difference in the real world. Granted, their impact can often be minimal or distorted; as Marx said, men make their history, but not just as they please. But from time to time, ideas can affect the course of society. It may be true that impersonal or accidental historical forces open and close windows of opportunity for ideas, but at those opportune times, humans act on the basis of the ideas, not the forces. To say that one form of society is better than another is to say that if its members recognize the difference, they will try to create the better and not the worse. We need not assume that ideas are all-powerful; the normative aspect of development can be significant even if it operates only some of the time.[18] A theory of change must, therefore, incorporate a theory of normative choice.

Such a theory cannot itself be nonnormative, however, because it must apply to our own choices as well as others'. It is all very well for us to explain others' moral choices in terms of their greed, their reptilian hindbrain, or their mothers having dropped them on their heads at birth, but we would not accept that as an explanation of our own behavior. Even if we saw, retrospectively, that such nonnormative factors had been governing our moral choices, we would still be free to ask the open question: "But is it right that I make reptilian moral decisions?" The question demands either a change of moral choice (and a consequent falsification of the reptile theory) or a change in the justification to a normative one. In short, if we are to treat our subjects as respectfully as ourselves, a theory of normative choice must capture the *normativeness* of their choices, not just the choices themselves. As Habermas puts it:

> Since the days of Max Weber [the value neutrality of the researcher] has been regarded as a virtue; however, even if one adopts this interpretation, the suspicion remains that legitimacy, the belief in legitimacy, and the willingness to comply with a legitimate order have something to do with motivation through 'good reasons'. But whether reasons are 'good reasons' can be ascertained only in the performative attitude of a *participant* in argumentation, and not through the neutral *observation* of what this or that participant in a discourse holds to be good reasons. . . . [One] might well want to know whether a certain party renounces obedience because the legitimacy of the state *is* empty, or whether other causes are at work (Habermas, 1979e:200).

Because people evaluate moral reasons in a performative attitude, even a scientific description of their choices (made in what Habermas terms the "objectivating attitude") must meet the moral reasons of the performative attitude on an equal footing.[19] The distinctive criteria of moral value must be approached on their own terms, not terms of scientific, objective validity.

Political development has always been a moral concept as well as an empirical one. Early work in this area was shamelessly explicit in its identification of "development" with "good." Early advocates of "civilization" and "progress" reflected what still continues as a basic desideratum of change—that it be to something better. Currently, the ethnocentric and even imperialistic excesses of our intellectual ancestors induce us to disguise our shameful normative ambitions behind the fig leaves of "modernization," "Westernization," and "change." No longer do societies develop—they only change, or become modern, or become like the West. But one can still just hear the collective murmur that it's a *good thing* they're doing it.

We may as well face the normative issues, because, like the

Victorians before us, we find that "not talking about it" just makes it emerge in more bizarre forms. Because political development is inherently a normative concept, attempts to circumvent, suppress, or disguise its normative aspects cannot succeed. In any case, the citizens of the developing world don't want a nonnormative theory of development; rather, they want a normatively grounded theory that speaks to *their* normative concerns. (The "developing world," of course, includes the potentially still-developing Western and Eastern worlds.) Political development "only" requires a normative theory that embraces these many, seemingly disparate ethical perspectives. This, then, is the challenge of normative grounding. Rather than avoid it, I propose we recognize its solution as a desideratum of development conceptions and see where this demand leads us.

A Brief Prospectus

The remaining chapters lay out a conception of political development that overcomes these theoretical challenges. This conception defines political development in terms of changes in political culture, not in terms of changes either in the political attitudes of individuals or in the empirical regularities of social interaction, although culture is closely related to both. As discussed in Chilton (1987), political culture consists of all publicly common ways of relating. These ways of relating, dealing with the same problems faced by systems of moral reasoning—how people are to relate to one another—are structured in the same manner as Kohlberg has found moral reasoning to be structured. (See Colby et al., 1983.) Thus political cultures may also be arranged in a sequence in which "higher" in the sequence means both "psychologically more integrated and differentiated" and "philosophically and morally more adequate." Development refers to the cognitive structure underlying the culture, however, not to the specific cultural content. A variety of cultures can exist at the same developmental stage. Locating political development in the cultural system admits several sources of change: change due to cognitive-developmental forces; change due to social inertia; and change due to hegemonic control over available cultural alternatives.

Methodology

General fields of intellectual inquiry can be divided into four theoretical levels along a continuum ranging from the most to the least theoretical issues. At the most abstract level are the general questions, problems, and/or theoretical desiderata that constrain the general field of discourse. At the second level are general approaches to answering these questions, meeting these problems, or satisfying these desiderata. Within such approaches lies the third level: theories attempting to explain or analyze particular elements of the general field of discourse. At the most specific level lie empirical tests of these theories, and exploratory case studies. These various levels are listed in Table 1 for three different fields of discourse: the field of social justice, and specifically John Rawls's (1971) approach; the field of genetic epistemology, specifically Jean Piaget's approach; and

Table 1. Four Levels of Theorization in Three Fields

Level/Subject	Social Justice	Genetic Epistemology	Political Development
1 Theoretical questions and/or criteria (constitute the field of discourse)	Justice as basic Universality Prescriptivity No reliance on specific theories of human nature	Origins of knowledge Basic functions of organisms	Five fundamental theoretical challenges to conceptions of political development
2 General way of meeting problems	The original position and the veil of ignorance	Developmental research	Examine cognitive basis of publicly common behavior
3 Specific theories	The two principles of justice (Rawls)	Structures and development (Piaget; Kohlberg)	Speculations advanced in the present work
4 Empirical tests and case studies	Applications of principles of justice to specific ethical problem areas, e.g., tolerance of the intolerant; civil disobedience; majority rule	Studies of the acquisition of knowledge in various areas, e.g., logic, space, time, morality	Döbert, Habermas, Hallpike, Hobhouse, Radding, Stokes, Wynn

the field of political development, specifically the approach taken in this and several related works.

For political development, the first level consists of the five fundamental theoretical challenges posed in this chapter, particularly the questions of normative grounding and the micro-macro connection. These challenges stand as the basic task of theoretical discourse, constraining the field of political development to approaches that meet them—or are at least capable of meeting them. Negatively, these challenges appear before development theorists as problems. Again and again, development theories are judged by, and fail because of, how they answer these questions. It is in this sense that I refer to them as "constituting the field of discourse." Development theories are those for which such questions are appropriate. Even if they are hard questions, we are still forced to consider them when we wish to evaluate what we have done. Positively, however, these challenges appear to us as guides to fruitful lines of analysis. By taking them seriously, we are directed to the core of theoretical difficulties. A proper understanding of the organization of the deep, central concepts of any field permits sure and flexible production of specific theories and inter-pretation of data. Once central theoretical problems are solved, applications are straightforward. Asking the right theoretical questions and insisting on their answers is, for that reason, a positive guide to fruitful research.[20]

The second level of this work is the way it engages these challenges. It does so by integrating the two approaches of genetic epistemology and symbolic interactionism. From genetic epistemology this work takes the general focus upon reasoning structures as an explanation of human behavior. "Normative grounding" and its consequence, "development," arise from the parallelism between the psychological equilibration of reasoning structures and the philosophical justification of reasons. From symbolic interactionism this work takes the general perspective of the social order as constructed and potentially mutual, although this mutuality may be coerced. A basically Parsonian trichotomy of personality system, cultural system, and social system is necessary to house the mutual construction properly, but once done, the micro-macro connection is apparent.[21] This work connects genetic epistemology and symbolic interactionism by emphasizing prescriptivity as a criterion of moral reasoning: by recognizing that morality cannot be simply a universalizable philosophy but must ultimately be carried into action.[22]

The third level is where specific theories are advanced to deal with specific problems in the general field of development. This work employs Kohlberg's theory of moral development—in my judgment the best-executed (and certainly the best-elaborated) genetic-epistemological theory of moral reasoning. I use this theory's sequence of moral reasoning stages to generate in Chapter 4 a developmental theory of cultures and institutional/social forms. Chapter 5 advances various theories about the nature of developmental dynamics, employing a variety of earlier analyses of how public commonness is created or inhibited.

The fourth level of this work consists of the examples advanced to validate the theories. The present work treats theoretical issues more than case studies, so the fourth level is not much in evidence here. There are, however, a surprising number of case studies that illustrate the use of moral development to explain political development. The most famous is Hobhouse's (1906) classic, *Morals in Evolution*. Though Hobhouse is weak theoretically, having had to ground his work on the inadequate Social Darwinism of his time, his basic outline of the moral codes in different civilizations has never been refuted (Kohlberg, 1981a:129). Other examples include: Radding's (1978, 1979, and 1985) extensive studies of reasoning in medieval society; Stokes's (1974) related study of the origins of nationalism; Hallpike's (1979) analysis of the effects of reasoning structures on various aspects of primitive society; Wynn's (1980) study of the necessity of certain cognitive structures for the production of certain tools by early hominids; and Döbert's (1981) complex analysis of the cultural regression represented by the medieval European witch craze.[23]

Because the four theoretical levels both support and discipline one another, the evaluation of the overall analytic framework is complex. Empirical evidence cannot by itself disprove a theory, because the evidence itself may not have been gathered properly.[24] At a higher level, the ultimate rejection of a theory cannot in and of itself force the abandonment of a general approach, as Kuhn (1970a) points out.[25] At a still higher level, even the abandonment of a general perspective will not necessarily make the basic questions of a field less relevant.[26] Research is thus incapable of proving or disproving in any categorical fashion the claims of any of these four levels.

Research should serve, instead, to examine and reexamine the different claims made at the four levels until they reach what Rawls (1971) calls "reflective equilibrium," a state in which each level supports and is supported by its neighbors.

This work concentrates primarily on levels one and two of Table 1. Its specific images of developmental stages and its specific theories of developmental dynamics are speculative—plausible to me, and certainly seriously intended, but still speculative. No case studies or empirical data are offered in support of these speculations, except a general claim of support from those works (Hobhouse et al.) cited.

Evaluation of the present work accordingly requires not a determination of its empirical accuracy but of its theoretical usefulness, where utility is judged not just by empirical accuracy but also by plausibility, suggestiveness, and theoretical coherence.[27] To anticipate the analysis, the issue is not whether political development is located in the cultural system, but whether it is useful to see it thus. The issue is not whether feudal Europe was a Stage 2 society, but whether specialists in the period (e.g., Radding) find cognitive commonalities helpful in understanding medieval society. The issue is not whether public commonness exists, but whether useful theories of developmental dynamics naturally derive from this perspective. Theories are judged by their ability to predict and explain empirical phenomena; general perspectives are judged by their usefulness in suggesting theories.

Notes

1. Conversely, only in the theoretical labor of clarifying that principle can we overcome our blind reactions to our own historical circumstances.

2. The work gives no definition of political development. Subject index entries do appear for "development, definition of," "developmentalist model," and "development goals," but the last two do not refer to definitions, and the first refers to a simple definition of development (not political development) as the growth in GNP per capita.

3. The terms "development" and "political development" appear neither in Bensel's index nor his table of contents. Some articles with political development in their titles subsequently use the term not at all (e.g., Sollie, 1984; Dobelstein, 1985) or almost not at all (e.g., it is mentioned only once in Khalilzad, 1984-5, and Hope, 1985).

4. In his more recent work, Huntington (1987) appears to have reconciled himself to use of the term.

5. To draw a parallel with another field, psychologists have long battled over the concept of "self," finding these battles theoretically enlightening, not cause to abandon the term.

6. As I have argued in another context (Chilton, 1987), there are three general ways social scientists can obtain agreement (and, we hope, clarity) on theoretically central concepts: by consensus, by fiat, and by analysis.

Consensus, if it existed, would be the simplest method, but as the works cited in the text have repeatedly demonstrated, it doesn't exist. Furthermore, even if consensus were to exist, it still might not provide either conceptual clarity or empirical utility. In the same way as the camel is said to be a horse designed by a committee, consensus might only yield a concept awkward of result and/or incoherent with other, related concepts.

Fiat is not possible either, because we have no philosophical Leviathan to impose order on our conceptions. The normative connotations of political development are especially relevant here, because our professional search for a Leviathan of analytic frameworks is thus equivalent to a normative search, à la Hobbes, for a Leviathan of morality. (This connection between analytic frameworks and normative positions is lifted from Sheldon Wolin's, 1960:Chapter 8, fine analysis of Hobbes.) And, as in the case of consensus, agreement by fiat would not guarantee either the resulting concept's coherence within a larger theoretical framework or its utility in scientific explanation.

Agreement by analysis might be possible, however. "Analysis" here means a process of specifying generally accepted challenges to/demands on potential conceptions of political development. If such challenges exist, then candidate conceptions of political development can be assessed against them. The challenges can be used to discard some conceptions, to direct our attention to more promising conceptions, and—if political development is as central an organizing concept as it appears—to discover a uniquely satisfactory conception possessing both conceptual and empirical clarity. If the theoretical questions are indeed fundamental ones, this approach will provide theoretical coherence as well as agreement. This is the approach taken in this work.

7. The term "thing" connotes conceptual specificity, not physical existence.

8. I do not claim that this statement represents the limits of Huntington's vision—merely that the partial vision has been taken for the whole.

9. Goulet (1971) does present a fully elaborated conception of development.

10. Payne (1984:35-37) nicely characterizes such confusions

"allow[ing] hypotheses to become embedded in definitions."

11. The previous examples are all cited in Park (1984:54-55).

12. Contrast Park's (1984:46-48, 51-52, points 3 and 5) consciously "methodological individualist" argument that individuals should be the locus of development. Park does not, however, exclude the possibility that what develops is an emergent property of individuals not definable merely by aggregating them.

13. Stephen White (1977:31), citing Radkey (1950:57-63) and Levin (1973:89).

14. Elder and Cobb (1983:144-145) term the micro-macro problem one of "the most basic and perennial questions in political analysis."

15. (a) I avoid here the term "stages" of development, which connotes finite and discontinuous values. Though the concept of development proposed here is indeed a stage concept, that result should flow from the empirical nature of development, not from an imposed theoretical demand.

(b) Park (1984:43-44, 51, point 2) pushes for an ideal-type definition of political development (thus entailing the specification of the various states of development) as a reaction to those nonideal-type definitions that derive the nature of development empirically by contrasting what one thinks are developed societies to those one thinks are not.

16. Park (1984:52) makes this very point. His discussion is flawed in two respects, however. First, he apparently assumes that the so-called developed countries are "inappropriately termed 'developed'" (ibid). While he may be correct, he goes too far; the unsupported assumption does not belong in a list of conceptual desiderata. (Without arguing for this point, one can entertain the hypothetical possibility that Western society is the most developed, be it ever so flawed.) Second, Park excludes the possibility of "linear sequential" theories of development, preferring cyclical theories. Once again, his recognition of a possibility becomes, without support, a conceptual criterion.

17. Park (1984:45, 52, point 4) makes the related demand that any conception of development must be universally applicable.

18. I am indebted to Philip Abrams's Historical Sociology (1982) for clarifying my thinking in this area.

19. Habermas (1983:256): "Interpreters sacrifice the superiority of observers' privileged positions, since they are involved in the negotiation about validity claims. By taking part in communicative actions they accept an equal standing with those whose utterances they want to understand. . . . Within a communicative process, . . . there is no a priori decision as to who has to learn from whom in order to reach a common understanding." Also see Habermas's (1983) discussion of the evaluation of Kohlberg's theory through the "complementarity" between the performative and objectivating attitudes.

20. The fruitfulness of Newtonian physics, for example, was based on Newton's clear analysis of the concepts of space, time, mass, inertia, and acceleration.

21. See Chilton (1987). The trichotomy parallels Habermas's "universal pragmatics" trichotomy of validity claims (1979a), which parallelism lends support to the basic naturalness of the approach. Habermas (1979c) sketches a general theory of development similar to the present one.

22. Kohlberg's writings tend to emphasize the universality criterion, although such works as Kohlberg and Candee (1984) do argue that higher-stage moral reasoning is associated with greater behavioral execution.

23. These studies (except Hobhouse's) use Piaget's theory of moral development, not Kohlberg's.

24. The physicist who postulated the existence of the "weak force" saw eight experimental projects fail to find evidence for it before the ninth project did. "Never believe an experimental finding until it is confirmed by theory," was his theorist's dig at experimenters.

25. Theorists continued to attempt to explain the famous Michelson-Morley experiment in Newtonian terms until Einstein's relativistic perspective showed them a simpler way.

26. The basic philosophical questions about the nature of space and time were not changed by the shift from Newtonian to relativistic physics. It was the theoretical perspective that changed.

27. This discussion obviously leads us into the thickets of the philosophy of science, where debate continues about the criteria by which we may judge one theory or perspective or paradigm as better than another.

TWO

The Locus of Development, The Micro-Macro Connection, and Exact Specification

Political Culture Is the Locus of Development

This work will locate political development as change in the political culture. The concept of political culture is, however, in some theoretical confusion, so we will employ an idiosyncratic definition of it. I advance a definition strange to the reader because (a) previous definitions do not satisfy the standard criteria theorists place on the concept; (b) the definition set forth here does satisfy these demands; and (c) this definition also meets the theoretical requirements for conceptualizing political development.[1]

The social order is not real but constructed, constituted in the ways people relate to one another. Humans have invented a vast variety of ways they can relate to each other: as fellow citizens, as father and son, as robber and robbery victim, as colleague and colleague, as seller and purchaser, as writer and reader, and so on. Each life embraces numerous and quite disparate ways of relating to others.

What people commonly term institutions, mores, laws, customs, roles, languages (including slang and jargon), and lifestyles are, upon closer examination, all ways they relate to one another. Although people constantly reify institutions, saying "Congress raises taxes" or "the post office is so slow," only individuals act, never institutions. Institutions like Congress simply reflect a specific way people relate to one another: Congressional representatives to one another, the representatives to their constituents, and constituents to one

23

another in terms of a political system with the representatives doing those things.

There are several perspectives from which one can look at ways of relating, but not all are equally profitable. The least profitable is to look at them as specific behavioral responses to the objective social environment. This behaviorist approach has no natural ability to capture the flexibility and adaptiveness of a way in which people relate, where vastly different environments and behaviors can be handled in the same way of relating. Conversely, different people can respond quite differently to the same environment, because their cognitive structures differ from one another, as Piaget discovered long ago.[2] A somewhat better perspective is to look at ways of relating as "action systems," in Talcott Parsons's sense of action as intentional social behavior. The philosophical difficulties of establishing intentionality make this approach only partially satisfactory, however.[3]

The best perspective is to look at ways of relating in terms of reasoning structures. This perspective recognizes the prior agency of the social actor in making her* environment meaningful. The actor actively identifies and at the same time interconnects aspects of her environment.[4] Her cognitive activity in doing so and in deciding on action is called "reasoning." Ordinary discourse recognizes such a preliminary process: we ask people how they see things, why they did that, and how they came to that conclusion. Our understandings of our world are often seen as objective, because for the most part people share outlooks, and the role of reasoning is accordingly obscured. Its role is revealed instantly, however, when agreement breaks down.[5]

Fixed environments may eventually induce recurrent responses, but environmental changes quickly reveal these

---

*With the kind permission of the publisher, I use female pronouns throughout for the common gender. I find plural pronouns awkward to use, particularly in a work so concerned with distinguishing the isolated from the collective social actor; "he or she" and the like are awkward and intrusive; and alternation of gender requires the author to keep track of whether she is currently speaking of a female or male neuter. Since our language currently possesses no gender-free personal pronouns, the choice lies between the masculine and the feminine. I hope the reader will welcome this opportunity to discover, from her own reaction to the consistent use of the female common gender, the connotations of the alternative usage.

responses' foundation in reasoning. Bureaucrats, for example, appear to employ regular, mindless bureaucratic procedures. But even obedient clients can present problems calling for interpretation, and some clients, as Danet (1971) points out, also use extralegal appeals: sob stories, bribes, and even threats. Such appeals require the bureaucrat to re-reason her rote use of the rule-book by asking: "What is the value of following the rules when set against (for example) a monetary gain for myself?" The answer may appear obvious to the reader, but the long history of bureaucratic corruption shows it is not always obvious to bureaucrats. In short, any way of relating, including that represented by the most rule-bound bureaucracy, is founded on reasoning rather than fixed rules. Researchers must, therefore, inquire into people's understandings of their behavior—-the schemas they employ—rather than their behavior alone.

When people relate to one another, either directly (as when I meet you at a conference) or in terms of the "generalized other" (as when I write this with the reader in mind), each person may choose to relate in any of the numerous ways in her repertoire. Given this variety of possibilities, for communication to occur or for an institution to be constituted demands that the interaction employ a way of relating that is publicly common. Public commonness means two things: First, the way of relating must be common to the parties involved. Thus if you are so unfortunate as to be a high school student assigned to read this, my language and references will not be common to us both, and the result will certainly not be what I intend. Second, the way of relating must be publicly common—mutually understood as the basis of interaction and thus used by all actors to orient to one another (the public focus of orientation).[6] Thus the title of this book and the sources from which you obtained it all cue the mutual basis on which our interaction is to take place. Parsons and Shils (1951:16) refer to this public commonness as "complementarity of expectations."

The political culture of a collectivity is whatever way of relating is publicly common to that collectivity.[7]

It follows that a large, diverse collectivity may well have no political culture—may not, properly speaking, be a political culture. The concept of public commonness—the actual use in interaction of a way of relating—makes analysts more aware of who does and who does not "participate in the culture." Even in such a highly selective and self-conscious institution as Congress, for example, certain members exhibit inappropriate behavior. Social science must differentiate a member of Congress's strategic power, available to all 535 members, from participation in Congress's dominant culture, which may be shared by only 534, or 533, etc. Nothing guarantees that any given agglomeration of people will have a culture. If, as in times of turmoil or rebellion, there is no such shared understanding, then no culture exists. Such times are commonly referred to as times of "cultural breakdown."

We call "subcultures" those ways of relating that are publicly common to a subgroup and that supplement rather than supplant the superordinate culture. If they do seek to supplant the superordinate culture, such cultures are called revolutionary (or deviant, depending on one's sympathies) cultures, not subcultures.

Following, and somewhat revising, Parsons's trichotomy of systems, this work distinguishes the individual system, the cultural system, and the social system. The individual system consists of those properties that characterize individuals considered in isolation (that is, without reference to their relationship to other individuals), and simple aggregates of those individual-level properties. The cultural system consists of all publicly common ways of relating. The social system consists of all objective regularities of interaction. A parallel trichotomy is made by Habermas (1979a) as a division among the linguistic domains corresponding to the validity claims of truthfulness, rightness, and truth. The claim of truthfulness is characteristic of the individual in isolation (that is, in the individual system), since no intersubjective standard of truth is involved. The claim of truth can be applied to objective descriptions of social interactions (that is, the social system): is in fact such-and-such a pattern observed or not? The claim of rightness applies only to the terms of people's mutual understanding of how the behavior (linguistic or otherwise) fits into their shared framework of interaction (that is, their cultural relationship).

The cultural and social systems differ in that the cultural system has normative significance, understood in Habermas's (1979a) "performative mode," and the social system has objective patterns of interaction, understood in Habermas's (1979a) "objective mode."[8] The cultural system is prescriptive, and its prescriptions are subject to moral evaluation; the social system is descriptive, and its descriptions are subject to scientific evaluation. The social system may result from, but can never contain, the human meaning of a normatively significant, publicly common way of relating. The cultural system can generate, but is not itself, regular patterns of social interaction.

The cultural and individual systems differ in that the individual system involves self-expressions, without necessary cognizance of others' perspectives, while the cultural system involves the establishment of interpersonal comprehension and intersubjective agreement. Individual system expressions may arise from, but are not the same as, the cultural system requirements of comprehension and agreement. The cultural modes of comprehension and agreement may give scope to, but are not governed by, individual system expressions.

This analytical division among the three systems is necessary to allow theoretical recognition of each system's distinct characteristics, especially its distinct dynamic processes. The theory therefore rigidly maintains the analytical separation of the systems in order to keep open methodologically the possibility of their differing. The distinction between individual and cultural systems, for example, allows a theoretical recognition of value dissensus and the associated breakdown of culture. Each individual knows many alternative ways of relating, among which one (not necessarily the same for every person) will be regarded as most preferred. These preferences can exist independently of social interaction, where any given way of relating may or not be publicly common. Individual system changes may not be reflected in cultural changes; changes that I experience, reflected in my self-expressions, may not directly affect the relationship we establish. And even if they do affect it, they do so in ways that depend on the interaction of our joint efforts.[9] In the context of defining development there is a special danger of unwittingly substituting theories of individual development for theories of cultural development.

The distinction between cultural and social systems allows a theoretical recognition of social system change as an independent source of cultural change. Regular patterns can become part of the cultural system simply by being recognized and desired as a point of cultural orientation—a way of creating meaning out of the jumble of life. For example, the installation of an office watercooler may, by affecting the objective pattern of people's interactions, create a new cultural object: "the 10 a.m. watercooler group." This phrase points to, makes meaningful, and thereby maintains the way the group members relate to one another. It crystallizes and raises to general consciousness a recognition of what they share, thus creating a cultural artifact out of a social system regularity. The social system force that creates the original regularity of interaction is simply thirst; the cultural object, however, once it is established, is maintained by the distinctive cultural forces of group solidarity, mutual expectations, anticipated reactions, and so on. Looking at this difference from the opposite perspective, the empirical regularities of interaction may, if unsupported by cultural understandings, break apart under the slightest accidental environmental pressure. For example, if the 10 a.m. watercooler crowd gathered only to slake their 10 a.m. thirst, they would disband if the watercooler were broken.

Political development is defined in this work as a specific form of change in the political culture of a society. The political cultural system, not the individual or social systems, is the locus of development. Of course, not all changes of the political culture are development; Chapters 3 and 4 describe what specific changes constitute development.

This position contrasts with many earlier proposals to locate development in the individual system. Such proposals saw development as the action of developed people in a society, and characterized developed people variously as economic entrepreneurs or high achievers (Schumpeter, 1949; Hagen, 1962; McClelland, 1976); as political participants (Almond and Verba, 1963); as experiencing unsatisfied higher needs (Aronoff, 1967, and, less explicitly, Maslow, 1954); and so on. Such theories locate development in the individual system and do not specify how these various isolated characteristics create different social organization or how they are virtues to be emulated.[10] They accordingly founder on the rocks of the micro-macro connection and/or of normative grounding. Development lies in how people coordinate their relations with one another—how they interact; it does not lie in individual, isolated virtue.

The social system also cannot be the locus of development because, as noted earlier, empirical regularities of interaction can alter quite readily if they are not actively maintained by the participants' cultural agreement. We cannot consider the arbitrary, vagrant patterns of noncultural interaction as the stuff of political development.

The Micro-Macro Connection

Although the individual, cultural, and social systems are analytically distinct, they can interact. Beliefs about which ways of relating are publicly common link the individual and cultural systems. On the one hand, such beliefs are part of the individual system because they are held by individuals. On the other hand, such beliefs are part of the cultural system because, to the extent that they are in fact shared, they are its actual expression.

Researchers can thus examine these beliefs from the perspective of either system. As part of the individual system, these beliefs are like any psychic phenomenon. Researchers can examine their origins and dynamics, their variation within the population, and so on. These are the concerns of conflict-oriented symbolic interactionism (e.g., Kemeny, 1976), which explores differences in individual beliefs about the operant cultural system. As part of the cultural system, these beliefs stem from and express a common cultural system, not individual idiosyncrasies. Researchers can examine the origins of these beliefs in socialization and hegemonic control of the culture, the beliefs' internal structure (e.g., as role systems), and so on. These are the concerns of role theory and of consensus-oriented symbolic interactionism (e.g., Hewitt, 1979), which explore the nature of, and the cues eliciting usage of, the operant cultural system.

People's normative evaluations of their culture are an especially important link between the individual and cultural systems. On the one hand, such evaluations are part of the individual system: one person's evaluation does not depend of necessity upon another person's. On the other hand, shared evaluations known to be shared are part of the cultural system. If the evaluations are positive, this provides an enormous source of legitimacy for the culture, quite beyond the aggregation of isolated beliefs in its legitimacy. If the evaluations are negative, this may result in a cultural change (or a "deviant" culture). For example, if the population at large becomes convinced that the tax system is unfair, then an underground economy may spring up to avoid the system.

Shared negative evaluations cannot by themselves constitute a culture, however. Rejection of one cultural system does not mean creation of a new one; as politicians say, you can't beat somebody with nobody. Shared knowledge that many people reject the existing culture may encourage a search for a counterculture, but it does not produce one. For example, some people observe the increasing proportion of "independent" voters and call for an Independent Party. But "independent" voters are not all of a kind: they include the ignorant, the passive, the disaffected, anarcho-syndicalists, and so on. Mere shared negative valence does not produce a culture.

Although the cultural and social systems are distinguished, they are also linked. Just as individual beliefs about the cultural system link the individual and cultural systems, so do institutions[11] link the cultural and social systems. On the one hand, institutions are part of the cultural system because they embody publicly common ways of relating. On the other hand, institutions are part of the social system because they give rise to empirically regular patterns of interaction.[12]

Researchers can thus examine institutions from the perspective of either system. As part of the cultural system, institutions can be studied phenomenologically to determine what publicly common, normative expectations about relationships they represent. The analytical-theoretical focus is therefore on the nature of these expectations and only secondarily on the resulting behavior. For example, Fenno (1978) and Kingdon (1973) adopt this perspective when they describe in phenomenological terms how members of Congress relate to their constituents (Fenno) and to other members (Kingdon). As part of the social system, institutions can be studied empirically to determine their regular patterns of interaction. The analytical-theoretical focus is therefore on what regularities of behavior can be detected, and only secondarily on what normative expectations underlie them. White, Boorman, and Breiger (1975) and Chilton (1977) adopt this latter perspective when they attempt to describe the empirical relationships within various collectivities.

Let us look more closely at this form of analysis, because it is rare to have empirical regularities of interaction studied independently of prior cultural categories. White, Boorman, and Breiger (1975) analyzed Sampson's (1978) monastery data and discovered an objective sociometric pattern of three groups. Two of these were mutually exclusive: with virtually no exceptions, members had feelings of liking and esteem for their own group's members, and feelings of antagonism and disesteem for the other group's members.[13] White, Boorman, and Brieger's "blockmodeling" approach reduces the sociomatrices to three basic elements: a set of roles (e.g., for the monastery, the roles "Loyal Opposition member" and "Young Turks member"); role assignments for the actors (e.g., the assignment of each monk to one of the two groups); and role interaction patterns (e.g., a 2x2 role interaction matrix showing that positive relations lie within, and not between, the two groups). This role interpretation employs cultural system language, but nevertheless it remains part of the social system. It characterizes objective patterns of interaction, not necessarily any shared subjective interpretations producing those patterns.

White, Boorman, and Breiger's approach attempts to deduce a society's culture from its social structure. Despite its clear success in many cases, however, analysts must recognize the problematic nature of that deduction, because not all regular patterns of interaction stem from the cultural system. As the authors state it, "social structure is regularities in the patterns of relations among concrete entities; it is *not* a harmony among abstract norms and values" (White, Boorman, and Breiger, 1975:733).

Despite the distinctions among the three systems, their linkages do allow us to say that a given political culture induces corresponding individual and social systems. "Induces" does not mean that this correspondence must always hold, but rather that (a) one can easily conceive of the individual and social systems that would correspond in an ideal-typical sense to the political culture, and (b) there do exist some forces equilibrating the three systems. These forces are summarized in Figure 1.

First, individuals would be socialized. Socialization in this context means training in the culture's ways of relating and the discovery that these are publicly common. Children may initially be treated in a way different from adults, but the child is ultimately taught and expected to relate to others in the culture's way. The child also has an opportunity to witness adult interactions and learn from them. And, of course, some cultures have special institutions devoted to the teaching of children. The recent focus on "the hidden curriculum" is based

Figure 1. The "Steady-State Society"

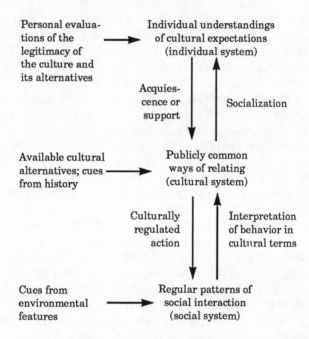

on a recognition that while schools may not directly teach certain ways of relating, the power relationships embodied in schools provide an implicit lesson.[14]

Second, social actors would acquiesce in or even support the cultural way of relating by employing it to regulate their interactions. The perpetuation of a political culture demands only acquiescence—that is, a continued willingness (whether liked or not) to relate to others in the way of the political culture. All that is required is for people to choose that way of relating and to believe in its public commonness. However, acquiescence provides no strong support for a culture: acquiescence to one culture may be replaced easily by acquiescence to another through a widespread indifference to (or even active dislike for) the former. To say that a person only acquiesces in the culture implies that preferable alternatives exist. To say that a person supports the culture, on the other hand, implies that she will not readily abandon it.[15]

Third, the cultural system creates regular behavior patterns in the very expression of cultural behavior by actors. Such regular patterns will only be found in a stable culture and stable environment in which actors repeatedly interact the same way. As the environment becomes more variable, social scientists will discover regular behavior patterns only with models that are informed by the underlying cultural reasoning: less sophisticated models based on coldly literal observation of physical motion become increasingly inappropriate.

Finally, the regular patterns of the social system provide ready material for social actors to assign them cultural significance. When created by the cultural system in the first place, these regularities are of course immediately interpretable in its terms. If not created by the cultural system, however (as in the example of the thirsty workers gathering at the watercooler), the regular patterns become subject to "projective" interpretation in cultural or other terms. ("Projective" is used here in the sense of projective tests.) Thus the objective fact of a worker's unemployment may be given various interpretations: "the penalty of an unproductive workforce" (by employers); "a technical readjustment" (by economists); "the first signs of capitalist breakdown" (by radicals); or even "God's punishment of you for hitting me" (by the worker's spouse). This variety of possible explanations provides the raw material for the eventual production, as hegemonic and other general forces come into play, of a culturally approved explanation.

It is convenient to start our analysis with the above "steady-state" image of an ideal-typical society in which the individual, cultural, and social systems are equilibrated to one another. This image will later allow us to examine the cultural forms that correspond to stages of individual development, thereby producing the required conception of political development. The ideal-typical society is only an analytical device, a tool for examining intersystem forces and a benchmark against which disequilibrium can be measured. The conception of political development presented here is thus simultaneously of stasis and of change. It attempts to show how cultures remain stable and also how they change. Since social equilibrium is maintained through the four dynamic social processes, we will be able to study social change in terms of alterations in these dynamic processes.

By locating culture between the individual and social systems, by identifying how individual beliefs about the cultural system link the individual and cultural systems, by identifying how institutions link the cultural and social systems, and by identifying the dynamic forces by which each system affects the adjoining system(s), the problem of the micro-macro connection is solved. When I say "solved," however, I mean only that the theoretical framework presented above "contains" or "tames" the problem by showing what specific modes of analysis are required to discover the micro-macro linkages at work in any specific society. Each society will have its own history, its own population, its own constraints of current custom, environment, and hegemonic control. Each society will accordingly present different research tasks, different developmental problems and, more generally, different trajectories of change. That the present perspective recognizes this variation is a virtue, not a liability.[16]

Exact Specification

Have we confused political development with its causes, consequences, correlates, or constituents? For the first three of these the answer is clearly no. We have defined development directly, not indirectly as the cause of some identified consequence, the consequence of some identified cause, or the correlate of some other identified social entity. Whether this is the right definition of development is not at issue here; that is a matter for this work as a whole. The only issue is whether the definition is direct or indirect.

Does the definition point to what is only a constituent aspect of development, however? Is the definition unduly limiting—for example, by excluding changes in material and aesthetic culture? This is a harder problem, but the answer still appears to be no. First, the concept of "political" in political development and political culture has been drawn widely enough to embrace every social form through which people relate to one another: political, legal, economic, religious, and general social institutions. Second, the requirement of normative grounding limits us to human relationships. We can evaluate material objects as functional or dysfunctional, but we cannot evaluate them as morally good or bad. The normative evaluation inheres in the human relationship the objects are to serve, not in the objects themselves. Similarly, we can evaluate artistic productions as aesthetically pleasing or displeasing, but we cannot evaluate them morally. While art may play a part in human relationships, any normative evaluation must be of the relationship, not of the art.

Notes

1. See Chilton (1987) for a detailed discussion and justification of this definition of political culture. Points (a) and (b) are made in ibid. Point (c) is merely another reason for using the definition given here, but it is not mentioned in ibid. It is interesting and reassuring that the theoretical criteria for political culture conceptions force the creation of a concept that turns out also to be necessary to overcome the rather different theoretical challenges to political development conceptions.

2. Even one person could evidence widely different responses as her cognitive structures changed. This variation of response may arise even over such obvious issues as whether liquid poured into a different container maintains its weight and volume.

3. The concept of intention immediately confronts the theorist with all the possible gradations of intentionality between "complete" and "none," e.g., Freudian slips, more-or-less unintended consequences, and so on.

4. "Aspects of her environment" sounds like the actor's recognition of objective elements, but in fact the aspects are themselves constructed by the actor. The processes of identification, interconnection, and meaning-making are simultaneous effects of assimilating the world to the cognitive structure. I will point out, without further discussion, that this approach might be usefully applied to the philosophical problems surrounding intentionality.

5. It is the charm of genetic epistemology that asking dumb questions reveals reasoning differences that no one imagined could exist.

6. Brown (1977:1) recognizes this characteristic of culture when he includes "the *foci* of identification and loyalty" (my emphasis) and "political . . . expectations" in his definition of political culture. Note that "public" does not mean "official." Widespread bribery may in certain countries be "public"—that is, adopted without discussion and with perfect understanding by all concerned in any transaction—even as it is "officially" condemned.

7. As used in this work, political culture embraces all aspects of interpersonal culture. It is distinguished from material culture, which concerns how people relate to their physical world, but not from economic culture or social culture. Note how this broad approach to political culture is necessarily similar to this work's broad approach to political development.

8. The social system thus includes unintended consequences.

9. For example, the changes that occur in a marriage are not simply the vector sum of the changes in the spouses but arise as a consequence of what new, organic relationship the spouses can create given their individual changes.

10. For example, David McClelland (personal communication) has said that he does not especially enjoy the company of people with the highest levels of n Ach.

11. The more general term would be "social forms," but it is awkward. I use "institutions."

12. As Habermas (1983:253) expresses this, "Any meaningful expression . . . can be bifocally identified, both as an observable event and as an understandable objectification of meaning."

13. The third group was an outcast group, disliked and disesteemed by both other groups.

14. See Overly (1970) and Kohlberg (1981) for a description of the hidden curriculum.

15. The sources of acquiescence and support lie to some extent in cognitive dynamics, which are discussed in Chapter 3, and the implications of these cognitive dynamics for cultural change are discussed in Chapter 5.

16. That each society must be understood within its unique historical circumstances, regardless of the overall theoretical framework we employ, is a point made at length by Abrams (1982), especially in his preface.

THREE

Normative Justification

Ways of Relating Constitute Ethical Systems

Reasoning about how one is to relate to others is moral reasoning, because any specific way of relating constitutes a practical answer to the basic question of moral theory: "How are we to take others' claims into account—what claims, in what way, and to what extent?"[1] This is not to say that all reasoning is of equal moral significance or requires equal deliberation. Clearly some judgments, e.g., stepping out of someone's path on a sidewalk, require little thought or effort, and actors may not often consider such ways of relating in moral terms. Nevertheless, morality is concerned at root with how people treat one another, so however banal the issue, the point remains that a decision is made.

To establish a certain way of relating as a culture is therefore a moral act, because one must justify the culture's implicit claim about how people should treat one another. A claim that people are to relate to one another in such-and-such a manner must be redeemed by normative argument and so, as Chapter 1's discussion of the challenge of normative grounding concludes, the normative issues raised by a theory of development must thus be considered.[2] As Monti (1982:241-242) puts it, "Public policies are essentially moral projects involving the total ethos of a culture and society . . . *ethics is the coordinating center of this public moral dialogue.*" It is in this sense that Habermas's validity claim of rightness is a normative claim as well as a practical one. Habermas (1979a:3) notes that communication can occur given only the (minimal) claim of mutual comprehension, but that in addition, any communication also makes the (maximal) implicit claim that the framework of communication treats the interlocutors morally.

An extensive body of longitudinal, cross-cultural, and cross-sectional research has shown that the moral reasoning of individuals has Piagetian cognitive structure.[3] The following claims, all supported by that research, are relevant to the present argument:

1. Moral reasoning varies in its structure (the logical interrelationships of the concepts). There are six possible structures, called "stages."[4]

2. The stages can be hierarchically ordered such that each stage represents an integration and differentiation of the previous stage (Kohlberg, 1981, 1984a; Kohlberg, Levine, and Hewer, 1984a).[5]

3. Stages are acquired in hierarchical order, with no skipping of stages and no retrogression to lower stages (Colby et al., 1983).

4. Progression through the stages depends initially on the successive recognition of each stage's relativity to different moral concerns and perspectives and ultimately on an appropriate reorganization of that stage to embrace and coordinate those perspectives. Thus progression is not inevitable, but it is possible—for any person, at any stage, whenever she perceives such relativity (Kohlberg, 1981, 1984a).

5. The above statements apply uniformly to all societies (Kohlberg, 1981; Kohlberg, Levine, and Hewer, 1984a; Nisan and Kohlberg, 1984; Snarey, Reimer, and Kohlberg, 1984; Weinreich, 1977; Edwards, 1975; Turiel, Edwards, and Kohlberg, 1978).[6]

The research can support these strong claims because it studies the structure of moral reasoning, not the content. Let us examine this distinction more clearly. One stage of moral reasoning (called "Stage 3" in Kohlberg's work) involves a "Golden Rule" maintenance of interpersonal relations through mutual role-taking. Consider the following two hypothetical Stage 3 answers to the question of whether a judge should give jail terms to conscientious objectors: (a) "The judge should put them in jail because that's what's expected of judges"; or (b)

"The judge should put herself in the conscientious objector's place and have a heart." In both answers the reasoning is structured in terms of the maintenance of good interpersonal relations and mutual role-taking. The conclusions drawn are opposite and the concerns brought to bear are different, of course, but these content differences stem from a very minor difference in thinking. The first answer tells the judge to role-take with other members of society, while the second answer tells her to role-take with the accused. The role-taking perspective is ambiguous in its application, and the diversity of content thus stems from the ambiguity of the simple Stage 3 structure. The distinction between content and structure is especially crucial in cross-cultural work, where content differences are extreme.[7]

Measurement Techniques

The Swiss psychologist Jean Piaget first discovered and outlined structural stages of cognitive development. Using a special clinical method, Piaget observed subjects (children) dealing with tasks requiring cognitive operations. By altering the tasks slightly and, for older children, by questioning them to learn their understanding of what they were doing, Piaget was able to discover the specific structures in which cognitive operations were organized and how these developed over time.

This method presents the researcher with two difficulties, however. First, it requires the researcher to assume nothing about her subjects' cognitive abilities, to ask them "dumb" questions, and to take their answers seriously. The lack of a fixed questionnaire makes the method's success entirely dependent on the skill and theoretical grasp of the researcher. Second, Piaget's method depends on controlled observation (e.g., interviews). These are not feasible in much social-scientific and especially historical research.

Kohlberg eliminated the first of these problems by using a standard set of moral dilemma stories (e.g., should a poor husband steal a drug necessary to save his wife's life) and follow-up probes (e.g., "What if the husband didn't love his wife?") to elicit his subjects' moral reasoning. The researcher can interview subjects individually, or administer the stories as a group written test. Responses are scored according to a detailed manual.[8]

This scoring system can also be applied to materials other than Kohlberg's standard moral judgment interview. Moral reasoning appears in many forms—inaugural addresses, letters, etc.—and can be scored wherever it appears. (Scoring reliability will vary, of course, depending on how explicitly and extensively the moral reasoning is set forth.) This permits social scientists and historians to conduct cognitive-structural analysis without interviewing their subjects.

The above methods measure the moral reasoning of individuals in isolation—that is, how they reason without reference to others' comprehension of their reasoning. The researcher's role is that of the perfect listener: having perfect understanding and making no judgments. A good interview thus elicits reasoning from the individual system, not the cultural system.

Cultural system reasoning is easy to find, however, since people employ it to communicate with and persuade each other within the context of their culture. Survey research's preoccupation with studying the individual's "true" opinion, carried over into Piaget's and Kohlberg's testing methods, has obscured the near-omnipresence of cultural reasoning.

Cultural materials containing such reasoning are already the subject of much research by social scientists not dependent on surveys. Such materials include presidential inaugural addresses (Yeager, 1974) and press conferences (McMillian and Ragan, 1983), Supreme Court decisions (Chesler, 1983), strike demands (Shorter and Tilly, 1974), theological arguments (Radding, 1979), children's stories (McClelland, 1976), congressional speeches (Rosenwasser, 1969), television shows (Lichter and Lichter, 1983), introductory college textbooks (Bertilson, Springer, and Fierke, 1982), public prayers (Medhurst, 1977), advertisements (Williamson, 1978), editorials (Sinclair, 1982), and newspaper stories (Van Dijk, 1983). Each of these categories of materials contains cultural moral reasoning insofar as it attempts to persuade of or to explain a desired course of action. Only the application of cognitive-structural analysis to these materials would be at all unusual.[9]

Researchers need not rely exclusively on secondary source materials, however. They may also elicit cultural moral reasoning directly by interviewing respondents in a public setting. Respondents could be asked to write persuasive appeals to other members of their culture. Or, respondents could be asked to study issues, meet in small groups, and decide as a group on the best argument for a course of action. Respondents could be interviewed about the reasoning behind their choices in Prisoner's Dilemma games. Respondents could be interviewed about their moral reasoning in front of their peers. In general, cultural reasoning is easier to study than private reasoning because the researcher can cast aside the classical experimental strictures to isolate the respondent. After all, if a respondent alters her responses in others' company, this indicates something about the group's conduct of politics in other settings.

The major difficulty in cultural research will be determining the intended audience, i.e., the cultural context within which such materials or responses are produced. In his inaugural speeches, whom was President Reagan addressing? His campaign staff? Campaign contributors? People who had voted for him? Those who didn't vote for him? Republicans? The nation as a whole? All human beings? Since the way of relating chosen will vary with the situation, the researcher must identify which culture is operative. In interviewing people directly, the researcher can easily find out how they see their imagined (or actual) audience. This task will be more difficult with historical records and, more generally, all expressions where the researcher can't question the participants. These problems are only methodological, however: culture as defined here is in principle measurable. Where researchers can question people directly, such measurement should also be quite straightforward in practice.

Kohlberg's Sequence of Moral Reasoning Stages

Biological structures adapt to their environment, Piaget says, through the two general processes of assimilation and accommodation.[10] In the broadest biological sense, assimilation is the organism's absorbing the world to provide sustenance for itself. For example, our own digestive systems are able to ingest and digest a great variety or things, all of which wind up as a few basic nutrients in our blood; our bodies assimilate the variety of the world to their own narrow requirements. In the broadest biological sense, accommodation refers to the structural elaboration necessary to permit the assimilation of the world's variety. While simple organisms merely pass seawater along a tube through their body, extracting whatever ready-made nutrients are present, our own bodies, though still basically tubes, deal with hard-to-extract nutrients by means of many specialized organs: teeth and tongue for masticating and extracting food; salivary glands, stomach, gall bladder, and pancreas for various chemical treatments; and of course legs and arms for chasing down and grabbing nutrients still on the hoof. Assimilation is the organism's reduction of the world's variety to the common denominator of food; accommodation is the organism's alteration of its own processing to better use the world's variety.

Cognitive development is one particular form of general biological adaptation in which assimilation and accommodation take special forms. Cognitive assimilation occurs as one construes reality; that is, re-presents it to oneself in terms of cognitive schemas. These schemas become successively more differentiated within themselves and integrated among themselves as reality proves resistant to the schemas' attempts to subdue it and they must accommodate to it.

Structures of moral reasoning assimilate moral reality both by being applied to new situations (e.g., how do the obligations of friendship apply to marriage, or to business partnerships, or to . . . ?) and by being applied to new moral perspectives (e.g., how do the obligations of friendship look from the point of view of one's friend, or from that of an acquaintance, or from . . . ?)

Structures of moral reasoning accommodate the complexities of moral reality by integrating the actor's moral perspective with those of other moral actors and by differentiating moral from nonmoral factors. This integration and differentiation is of previous reasoning structures, such that each reasoning structure simultaneously integrates and coordinates the perspectives of the previous stages and in turn serves as one of a set of elements coordinated and integrated by the subsequent stage. The resulting sequence of stages we term moral development.

Rather than pursue these abstract statements now, we will return later to a general discussion of their implications. I illustrate them here by presenting Kohlberg's six stages in the text below, from earliest (Stage 1) to latest (Stage 6).* The

---

*Pages 409–412 from *The Philosophy of Moral Development: Moral Stages and the Idea of Justice* by Lawrence Kohlberg. Copyright © 1981 by Lawrence Kohlberg. Reprinted by permission of Harper & Row, Publishers, Inc. (See also Kohlberg, 1984b.)

stages' definitions are supplemented by three parallel discussions. The first describes how each given stage overcomes the moral ambiguities in the previous stage.[11] This discussion will become important in later discussions of the theory's normative grounding.

The second discussion gives several examples of how the given stage appears in actual relationships. Kohlberg rightly takes pains to base his theory on structure rather than content, since cross-cultural validity demands such abstractness, but this chapter concerns how the cognitive stages appear in actual social relationships. Because structure does not determine content, many relationships are possible at each stage; the supplementary discussion gives a limited variety of specific relationships associated with each level. The examples given are not exhaustive of the ways of relating possible at each stage and, indeed, neglect non-Western cultures. For example, the Japanese relationships of *giri* and *on*, described by Benedict (1946), are not discussed here. I emphasize these limitations in order to preserve the theoretical strength of this approach, even

Table 2. **Speculative Classification of Cultural Stages**

Kohlberg's Descriptive Title	Interpersonal Relations/ Forms of Influence
1 Punishment and obedience ("might makes right")	Domination; physical compulsion; threats; seizure by force; extortion
2 Individual instrumental purpose and exchange ("what's in it for me?")	Barter and trading; deterrence by revenge; bribery; corvee labor; prebend; curses; feudal fealty and vassalage
3 Mutual interpersonal expectations, relationships, and conformity (the concrete Golden Rule)	Friendship; *compadrazgo*; romantic or courtly love
4 Social system and conscience maintenance ("law and order")	Mutual support of moral system
5 Prior rights and social contract or utility	Mutual respect; rational debate, fair competition, and scientific testing
6 Universal ethical principles (the second-order Golden Rule)	*Satyagraha; agape*; undistorted communicative action; mutual care

at the expense of highlighting the present chapter's limits. Specialists in other cultures can use this approach to broaden social scientists' understanding of the cultural variety possible at each stage.[12] Despite this caveat, the reader will see that the ways of relating mentioned, especially those at the lower stages, do appear in cultures worldwide. Table 2 summarizes the relationships (and/or forms of interpersonal influence) associated with each of Kohlberg's stages.

The third and last discussion describes the problems to which the given stage is subject.[13] This discussion motivates the later description of how the next stage overcomes these problems. The discussion also shows part of the psychological theory of what motivates development beyond the given stage.

It is well to begin this journey through the stages by putting ourselves at the same simple reasoning level as the Stage 1 reasoner:

Level A. Preconventional Level

Stage 1. The Stage of Punishment and Obedience

Content

Right is literal obedience to rules and authority, avoiding punishment, and not doing physical harm.

1. What is right is to avoid breaking rules, to obey for obedience' sake, and to avoid doing physical damage to people and property.
2. The reasons for doing right are avoidance of punishment and the superior power of authorities.

Social Perspective

This stage takes an egocentric point of view. A person at this stage doesn't consider the interests of others or recognize they differ from actor's, and doesn't relate two points of view. Actions are judged in terms of physical consequences rather than in terms of psychological interests of others. Authority's perspective is confused with one's own (Kohlberg, 1981:409).[14]

Stage 1 may be thought of as the "might makes right" stage: might makes right not with the resentful, cynical connotation that higher-stage reasoners bring to the phrase, but with the child's simple belief that right simply is what authorities— parents, police officers, older children—tell one to do. So when we think about Stage 1, we mustn't think too hard. If we just keep our thinking "real simple," the stage will be clear.

At Stage 1, interpersonal relations may be based on simple domination, physical compulsion, and/or threats. Sandlot bullies and their victims relate at this level.[15]

The problem with Stage 1 reasoning is that it cannot handle how equals are to relate. If neither is the authority or "big person," how do they know who is right? Furthermore, there are severe limitations on a moral authority that rests on the unthinking willingness of another to accept rewards and punishments as the immanent signs of the inherent goodness and badness of acts. Once the Stage 1 reasoner is able to differentiate the reward or punishment following an act from the goodness or badness of the act, she discovers that in many circumstances she can gain rewards or avoid punishments by such techniques as lying, running away, or doing things where authority can't see. In addition, such differentiation also makes apparent the many possibilities for revenge, even by a "weaker" person (e.g., puncturing tires; breaking windows). Authorities accordingly have severe limitations on what they can command, whether Stage 1 recognizes these limitations or not.

These problems are resolved at:

Stage 2. The Stage of Individual Instrumental Purpose and Exchange

Content

Right is serving one's own or other's needs and making fair deals in terms of concrete exchange.

1. What is right is following rules when it is to someone's immediate interest. Right is acting to meet one's own interests and needs and letting others do the same. Right is also what is fair; that is, what is an equal exchange, a deal, an agreement.
2. The reason for doing right is to serve one's own needs or interests in a world where one must recognize that other people have their interests, too.

Social Perspective

This stage takes a concrete individualistic perspective. A person at this stage separates own interests and points of view

from those of authorities and others. He or she is aware
everybody has individual interests to pursue and these
conflict, so that right is relative (in the concrete individualistic
sense). The person integrates or relates conflicting individual
interests to one another through instrumental exchange of
services, through instrumental need for the other and the
other's goodwill, or through fairness giving each person the
same amount (Kohlberg, 1981:409-410).

At Stage 2 it becomes clear how equals are to relate; in
effect, their equal autonomy makes everyone equal, and people
have to buy each other's cooperation. If cooperation isn't bought
but commanded, then revenge can be taken. "An eye for an eye
and a tooth for a tooth" is this element of Stage 2 reasoning. The
"problems" of Stage 1 are now recognized in Stage 2 as simple
facts. Big people do indeed have problems getting little people to
do things, and little people do know all the ways to get out of
being dominated or to make the dominator pay a price. This is
the stage where children learn to deal with bullies by standing
up to them.

In Stage 2 there are a greater variety of interpersonal
relationship names, but of course all are structurally equivalent. Stage 2's demand for positive reciprocity of values leads to
relationships of barter and trading. The marketplace, in which
goods are willingly traded by mutual consent of the parties
rather than seized by the stronger party, becomes possible at
Stage 2. Positive reciprocity underlies bribery, which is a moral
act at Stage 2, of course; the term itself connotes the judgment
of a perspective above Stage 2. Positive reciprocity also allows
corvee labor (vassal service to a lord in exchange for the lord's
protection) and prebend (a lord's maintenance in his household
of a vassal in exchange for that vassal's generally
administrative service).[16] Stage 2's demand for negative
reciprocity leads to systems of deterrence by revenge, including,
where physical punishment is not feasible, curses.

Despite these notable advances over Stage 1 relationships,
there are still problems with Stage 2. One problem is that
people have to have things to trade: if I don't have something
immediately at hand to offer you, it's unclear how we can do
business. Similarly (similar in structure, but opposite in
content), if I don't have a means of revenge upon you, it's
unclear how I can ensure we relate to each other as equals.
Further, my moral decisions vary with the abilities of my
partners: I am in a strong bargaining position vis-à-vis some

and a weak position vis-à-vis others. (See Poggi's, 1978:esp.55-56, description of such a phenomenon in feudal relations.) Thus Stage 2's moral claims will vary according to quite accidental variations in tactical strength. Finally, there is a problem of an infinite cycle of revenge—a feud in which neither side believes it has squared accounts with the other. Stage 2 offers no means of ending such feuds.

These problems are resolved at:

Level B. Conventional Level

Stage 3. The Stage of Mutual Interpersonal Expectations, Relationships, and Conformity

Content

The right is playing a good (nice) role, being concerned about the other people and their feelings, keeping loyalty and trust with partners, and being motivated to follow rules and expectations.

1. What is right is living up to what is expected by people close to one or what people generally expect of people in one's role as son, sister, friend, and so on. "Being good" is important and means having good motives, showing concern about others. It also means keeping mutual relationships, maintaining trust, loyalty, respect, and gratitude.
2. Reasons for doing right are needing to be good in one's own eyes and those of others, caring for others, and because if one puts oneself in the other person's place one would want good behavior from the self (Golden Rule).

Social Perspective

This stage takes the perspective of the individual in relationship to other individuals. A person at this stage is aware of shared feelings, agreements, and expectations, which take primacy over individual interests. The person relates points of view through the "concrete Golden Rule," putting oneself in the other person's shoes. He or she does not consider generalized "system" perspective (Kohlberg, 1981:410).

Stage 3 is the first stage at which an ideal relationship can be maintained exclusive of the behavior of the other person. It is the Golden Rule stage, where one orients to the relationship that is desired rather than the immediate behavior. In this way it resolves the problems of Stage 2. At Stage 3 it is no longer necessary to have immediate things to trade, because things given to the other are in the context of a continuing relationship in which some overall balance is expected to be struck. The overall advantages of the relationship itself outweigh temporary imbalances[17] and can compensate for many long-term imbalances. The problem of feuds is also eliminated, because both parties are oriented to the maintenance of an ideal relationship and hence can "turn the other cheek" to interrupt the cycle of revenge. For the same reason, the lack of a means of revenge (so important in Stage 2 for ensuring that one is not taken advantage of) is unimportant at Stage 3, because it is not revenge but the maintenance of a positive relationship that is desired.

Stage 3 interpersonal relations are mutually maintained, ideal relations. Friendship is of course the classic Stage 3 relationship; related relationships include that of the *patron* (or *compadre*) and apparently that of late-feudal fealty. Note, in support of this last claim, Bloch's (1961:228) reference to the "cancellation ceremony" that in the late feudal period was felt necessary to end a bond between lord and vassal. Such a ceremony would indicate a Stage 3 rather than Stage 2 relationship—only ideal bonds need a mutual dissolution; Stage 2's concrete bonds dissolve at either party's unilateral will. The chivalric code itself was a Stage 3 moral system, and the transition out of Stage 2 in the development of the chivalric code is mentioned in Bloch (1961:318): "But the sword thus consecrated, though it might still as a matter of course be drawn at need against his personal enemies or those of his lord, had been given to the knight first of all that he might place it in the service of good causes. . . . Thus a modification of vital importance was introduced into the old ideal of war for war's sake, or for the sake of gain." It is suggestive that this alteration in the chivalric code arose at the same time as the medieval concept of courtly love. In more recent times Stage 3 obligations are found in the institution of godparents. Among New Mexico Hispanics, for example, the *padrino* and *padrina* (godfather and godmother) would take their *hijado/hijala* (godson/goddaughter) into their home if the latter's natural parents died. The godparents and natural parents are *compadres* to one another. This relationship is less important to non-Hispanic Roman Catholics, for whom the godparent obligations concern primarily the godchild's spiritual welfare.[18]

Stage 3 has one major problem: it cannot coordinate multiple relationships.[19] Stage 3 relationships are fundamentally between two people, and the problem of coordinating any such relationship with other relationships is just that: a problem. To put the problem in concrete terms, recall Kohlberg's best-known moral dilemma story, in which Heinz's wife is dying of cancer and Heinz cannot pay for the drug that would save her. Should Heinz steal the drug? In this situation there are at least two dyadic relationships Heinz must consider: with his wife and with the druggist. Maintaining an ideal relationship with his wife means stealing the drug for her; maintaining one with the druggist means not stealing it. The central problem with Stage 3 is that it provides no coordinated means of resolving such conflicts. Stage 3 people come to a decision, of course, but the decisions are *ad hoc* and provide no generalizable means of resolving different conflicts.

Stages 1, 2, and 3 all share this characteristic of dealing solely with dyadic relationships. The stage transition beyond Stage 3 is therefore a major one, because it marks the transition between reasoning involving ways of two people relating and reasoning involving ways of people relating to one another in the context of their ways of relating to many people. Edwards (1975:511) also sees this as a major transition, speculating that "a boundary exists between stages 3 and 4. This boundary occurs, I would propose, because stage 3 is appropriate to the problems of social control and conflict resolution, whereas stage 4 contains assumptions more suitable for the model of a complex society." Gilligan (1977:489) notes that "[this] is the transition that has repeatedly been found to be problematic for women," and she advances the hypothesis that the higher-level stages (4-6 as opposed to 1-3) are handled "in a different voice" by women than by men, again implying the sharp break between the lower and upper stages. (See also Gilligan, 1982.)

The transition from Stage 3 to 4 is also significant because of the many parallels ("vertical decalages" is Piaget's term) between the first three stages (1, 2, and 3) and the last three stages (4, 5, and 6). In certain ways, Stage 4 is like Stage 1, Stage 5 is like Stage 2, and Stage 6 is like Stage 3. This can be seen in Kohlberg's scoring manual (Colby and Kohlberg, forthcoming), where the major scoring confusions are between

Stages 1, 2, and 3 and Stages 4, 5, and 6, respectively. Thus Colby et al. (1983:39) notes that the "[issue boundaries] of Stage 5 are again similar to the boundary pattern characterizing Stage 2 though the pattern is less pronounced at Stage 5 than at Stage 2." These parallels between the lower and upper stages will be noted in the discussion of the later stages.

To return to the descriptions, the problem noted above with Stage 3 is resolved by:

Stage 4. The Stage of Social System and Conscience Maintenance

Content

The right is doing one's duty in society, upholding the social order, and maintaining the welfare of society or the group.

1. What is right is fulfilling the actual duties to which one has agreed. Laws are to be upheld except in extreme cases where they conflict with other fixed social duties and rights. Right is also contributing to society, the group, or institution.
2. The reasons for doing right are to keep the institution going as a whole, self-respect or conscience as meeting one's defined obligations, or the consequences: "What if everyone did it?"

Social Perspective

This stage differentiates societal point of view from interpersonal agreement or motives. A person at this stage takes the viewpoint of the system, which defines roles and rules. He or she considers individual relations in terms of place in the system (Kohlberg, 1981:410-411).

Stage 4 resolves the problem of conflicting dyadic relationships by reference to an overarching sociomoral order to which the individual relationships are subordinated. The sociomoral order could take many forms (e.g., the Catholic Church; the Law; the Party Line; Social Custom), but it always takes a superordinate position vis-à-vis individual relationships. People at Stage 4 note, quite rightly as far as it goes, "We all have to obey the law or else there would be chaos." They recognize that Stage 3 reasoning does not regulate society as a whole and thus permits conflicts that are unresolvable at that stage.[20] It is important to recognize these definite strengths of Stage 4. As a stage it isn't as pretty or nice as Stage 3, but it is a real advance that solves a real problem.

The dramatic conflict in Sophocles' *Antigone* is between Stages 3 and 4, and the play's central moral lesson for the Greeks was the resolution of individual conflicts through an adherence to "God's law" (Watling, 1947). The play involves relationships among four principal characters: Creon, King of Thebes; the slain rebel Polynices, whose body Creon has forbidden to be honorably buried; Antigone, Polynices's sister, who is determined to bury Polynices; and Haemon, Creon's son and Antigone's fiance. Their conflicting relationships with Polynices lead Creon and Antigone into conflict, and their conflict induces conflicting loyalties for Haemon. He pleads with his father to respect the higher law governing these relationships,[21] and Creon's refusal brings death to Antigone, to Haemon, and to Creon's wife Eurydice. Creon's despair brings him knowledge too late, and the Chorus is left to draw the moral that "Of happiness the crown/ And chiefest part/ Is wisdom, and to hold/ The gods in awe./ This is the law." (Sophocles, 1947:162). In Stage 4 even kings are seen to be subject to the overarching law, a point Haemon argues directly. Stage 4 reasoning may be the most important invention of Athenian culture.

Stage 4 resembles Stage 1 because in both stages "the right" is defined by something or someone above oneself—by big people at Stage 1 and by a reified sociomoral order at Stage 4.

Stage 4 interpersonal relations are conducted within the framework of an overarching moral order. Rather than orienting directly to one another, Stage 4 actors share a mutual orientation to the same overarching moral system. Such moral systems bear the sanction of tradition, religion, or traditional authority—possibly all three. The possible relationships can therefore vary as widely as the range of possible overarching moral systems. People can relate as "patriotic, 100 percent Americans," as academic colleagues, as fellow Weberian bureaucrats, as co-religionists, etc. Any code can be used that subordinates separate relationships to its own maintenance.

Not accidentally, the problems inherent in Stage 4 resemble the problems inherent in Stage 1. At Stage 1, there were many avenues by which a "small" person could resist doing the right thing (i.e., what the big person wanted), and there was no way for equal people to relate to one another. At Stage 4, there are many ways people can resist the sociomoral order: to ensure that people obey the law requires a large investment of energy (e.g., in police agents or other forms of social control) and results in a very unpleasant, inflexible atmosphere. Furthermore, Stage 4 has no way of dealing with people from other sociomoral orders, including nonconformists within its own ranks. Good examples of this difficulty of dealing with other sociomoral orders can be drawn from the entire history of contacts between civilizations.

These problems, particularly the last, are the origin of an intermediate or transitional stage, formerly called "Stage 4 1/2," and most recently termed:

Level B/C. Transitional Level

This level is postconventional but not yet principled.

Content of Transition

At Stage 4 1/2, choice is personal and subjective. It is based on emotions, conscience is seen as arbitrary and relative, as are ideas such as "duty" and "morally right."

Transitional Social Perspective

At this stage, the perspective is that of an individual standing outside of his own society and considering himself as an individual making decisions without a generalized commitment or contract with society. One can pick and choose obligations, which are defined by particular societies, but one has no principles for such choice (Kohlberg, 1981:411).

Stage 4 1/2 has no systematic way to provide a society in which people want to participate and to whose rules they are willing to agree. This problem is solved at:

Level C. Postconventional and Principled Level

Moral decisions are generated from rights, values, or principles that are (or could be) agreeable to all individuals composing or creating a society designed to have fair and beneficial practices.

Stage 5. The Stage of Prior Rights and Social Contract or Utility

Content

The right is upholding the basic rights, values, and legal contracts of a society, even when they conflict with the concrete rules and laws of the group.

1. What is right is being aware of the fact that people hold a variety of values and opinions, that most values and rules are relative to one's group. These "relative" rules should usually be upheld, however, in the interest of impartiality and because they are the social contract. Some nonrelative values and rights such as life and liberty, however, must be upheld in any society and regardless of majority opinion.
2. Reasons for doing right are, in general, feeling obligated to obey the law because one has made a social contract to make and abide by laws for the good of all and to protect their own rights and the rights of others. Family, friendship, trust, and work obligations are also commitments or contracts freely entered into and entail respect for the rights of others. One is concerned that laws and duties be based on rational calculation of overall utility: "the greatest good for the greatest number."

Social Perspective

This stage takes a prior-to-society perspective—that of a rational individual aware of values and rights prior to social attachments and contracts. The person integrates perspectives by formal mechanisms of agreement, contract, objective impartiality, and due process. He or she considers the moral point of view and the legal point of view, recognizes they conflict, and finds it difficult to integrate them (Kohlberg, 1981:411-412).

Stage 5 resolves the Stage 4 and 4 1/2 problems, first by recognizing that people do indeed have different viewpoints, and second by setting up formal systems by which people have an opportunity to make their wishes known. This stage is the first to adequately justify minority rights, such as those provided in the Bill of Rights. Guarantees of freedom of speech, press, and association are explicit recognitions of people's autonomy prior to their voluntary association with the Stage 5 society.

Guarantees of freedom from unwarranted search and seizure are explicit recognitions of limits in the ways that Stage 5 society can intrude upon a person's autonomy.

Stage 5 resembles Stage 2 in its recognition of individual autonomy and its corresponding requirement that people's voluntary cooperation must be elicited. As Kohlberg (1981a:182) notes, social contract philosophers often deduce Stage 5 principles from the assumption of a Stage 2 reasoner having to deal with the problems of creating a society in which people will be willing to participate.

Stage 5 interpersonal relations are those of mutual respect for the participants' beliefs and desires, subject only to the mutually recognized criterion of rationality (meaning nonself-contradiction and empirical validity) and the mutually recognized goal of achieving stable, cooperative agreements. Stage 5 influence is based on compromise after rational debate—that is, once both parties are convinced of the rationality (the self-consistency and empirical groundedness) of their positions, they can compromise or decide on the basis of formally fair decision rules. (Civil liberties provide the opportunity for the initial inquiry into rationality.) This is the stage at which Almond and Verba's (1963) "participants" appear to relate.

Stage 5 does have its own problems, however. Stage 5 is a machine-like stage, in that people agree to formally fair "rules of the game" and take no responsibility for the consequences for anyone except themselves. Just as in Stage 2 there were people who had nothing to offer, so in Stage 5 there are people whose resources in making the rules are very small. Just as in Stage 2 there can arise endless cycles of revenge, so in Stage 5 people can be completely crushed in society's gears. There is no positive obligation of one person for another: the language of "rights" and "justice" exists apart from the language of "care" and "responsibility".[22] In Stage 5, people do not systematically take collective responsibility for the consequences of their collective actions, that is, they can dissociate themselves from the specific effects of the formally fair system.

These problems are resolved at:

Stage 6. The Stage of Universal Ethical Principles

Content

This stage assumes guidance by universal ethical principles that all humanity should follow.

1. Regarding what is right, Stage 6 is guided by universal ethical principles. Particular laws or social agreements are usually valid because they rest on such principles. When laws violate these principles, one acts in accordance with the principle. Principles are universal principles of justice: the equality of human rights and respect for the dignity of human beings as individuals. These are not merely values that are recognized, but are also principles used to generate particular decisions.

2. The reason for doing right is that, as a rational person, one has seen the validity of principles and has become committed to them.

Social Perspective

This stage takes the perspective of a moral point of view from which social arrangements derive or on which they are grounded. The perspective is that of any rational individual recognizing the nature of morality or the basic moral premise of respect for other persons as ends, not means (Kohlberg, 1981:412).

Stage 6 resembles Stage 3 in that both recognize the potential existence of an ideal way of relating, both recognize that it is important for the participants independently to choose to relate in this way, and both recognize that it is important in these ways of relating to examine the situation from more than one point of view. The difference between the two stages is that while Stage 3 concentrates only on maintaining the individual dyadic relationship, Stage 6 recognizes that a solution must be obtained at the level of all dyads simultaneously—i.e., at the level of society as a whole. Kohlberg (1981b:203-204), for example, terms the Stage 6 role-taking structure "a 'second-order' use of the Golden Rule."

In contrast to Stage 5, at Stage 6 people do take collective responsibility for the consequences of their collective action. Because the principles of justice are universalizable, each person in Stage 6 can face all other people and truly say, "I have done for you all it is possible for me to do under the conditions that I be able to say the same thing to all other people and that they be able to say the same to me."

Stage 6 interpersonal relations are those of mutual social

care. Christians name such a relationship *agape*; Gandhi's technique of *satyagraha* envisioned the same relationship with the opponent; Habermas's conception of undistorted communication envisions such a relationship; Rawls's debate in the Original Position, ditto. Stage 6 influence comes from the transformation of beliefs subsequent to mutually understood experience. While at Stage 5 agreements are reached as compromises without the parties altering their beliefs, at Stage 6 agreements are reached after a process deliberately designed to alter beliefs. Thus Gandhi wanted his opponents to change their minds, not simply capitulate; Rawls's concept of "reflective equilibrium" implies the possibility of cognitive change prior to equilibrium.

Higher is Better

The sequence of moral reasoning stages makes claims in two different areas simultaneously.

(1) To psychologists, the sequence makes claims both about the empirical nature of moral reasoning development and about the psychological origins of that development. The first claim is the baldly empirical one that everyone's moral reasoning moves through the specified sequence of stages in the specified manner (no retrogression, no skipping stages, and so on). The evidence for this has been cited above. At a more theoretical level, the claim is that development stems from the organism's successive attempts to create more equilibrated cognitive schemas through differentiation and integration of earlier schemas. Examination of the stage sequence clearly reveals such successive equilibration: Stage 4 integrates individual Stage 3 relationships and differentiates the latter into those corresponding or not corresponding to the former's overarching moral system. Stage 5, in turn, integrates conflicting Stage 4 perspectives through, for example, the conceptual device of the social contract, and differentiates Stage 4 claims into those upheld or not upheld in such a system. Similar arguments apply to the other transitions.

(2) To philosophers, the sequence lays claim to being a "rational reconstruction" of the ethical superiority of each stage over its predecessors (Habermas, 1983; Kohlberg, Levine, and Hewer, 1984b). Since Kant, deontological moral philosophers

have generally recognized that moral judgments must satisfy the criteria of universality and prescriptivity, even lacking agreement on what particular moral philosophy satisfies those criteria. As a sequence of moral positions, the six stages increasingly satisfy these criteria. Let us look at Stages 3, 4, and 5 as examples: Stage 4 defines general duties apart from the particular nature of relationships, thus broadening from Stage 3 the scope of moral obligations and making it more prescriptive than Stage 3 in its independence of relational particularities. Stage 5 defines duties in terms of a general recognition of others as moral agents, thus broadening once more the scope of obligation and making it more prescriptive than Stage 4 in its independence from the necessity of sharing absolute moral dicta. Again, similar arguments apply to the other transitions. The six stages accordingly form a hierarchy of moral adequacy: reasoning at higher levels is normatively better reasoning than at lower levels.[23]

Note particularly that the formal criteria concern only reasoning; they are not criteria either of the correctness of the decision made or of the moral worth of the person making it. Better reasoning presumably will lead to better decisions overall or in the long run, but the criteria do not guarantee that any specific decision will be correct. In fact, the structural ambiguity of earlier stages guarantees that nonmoral features of the situation can swing the decision arbitrarily among several alternatives, one of which will be the "correct" one. Even in common speech we dismiss such occurrences with the comment, "She made the right decision but for the wrong reasons." (Kohlberg and Candee, 1984, argue that higher-stage reasoning is correlated with a convergence in actual choice.)

We also cannot judge the moral worth of the people making the decisions. Although we can take action to ensure just treatment for all, to restrain people from unjust action, and to encourage better reasoning, it is pointless to blame people for employing the particular moral reasoning structure they possess. All people attempt to be moral in the sense that they understand the term. The just claims of people reasoning at higher stages are the same—must be the same, by the universality criterion—as the just claims of people reasoning at lower stages. That the latter may be unable fully to articulate these claims and may not respect their application to others does not negate their right to have them respected. Correlatively, the equal respect we must give to everyone's moral claims does not imply equal respect for all claims. The criteria do not demand that we respect a Hitler's nonuniversalizable claim to exterminate Jews.

Kohlberg's theory of moral reasoning stages is an individual-level theory and, like the individual-level theories listed in Chapter 2, it suggests what Kohlberg (1981a:128) himself has called "a mild doctrine of social evolutionism." But even if we accept Kohlberg's claim that his work is normatively grounded as a theory of individual moral development, we must still investigate the normative grounding of our related theory of political development. Recall that political development was defined in Chapter 2 as specific characteristics of the political culture; recall that political culture consists of all publicly common ways of relating; and recall that ways of relating are undergirded by moral reasoning. Accordingly, political cultures themselves have the cognitive structures of moral reasoning and can be similarly arranged in a hierarchy of moral adequacy. The stages of moral reasoning show the structure of hypothetical moralizing; the corresponding stages of political culture show the structure of that moral reasoning underlying the publicly common way of relating. Because moral reasoning underlies both cultural and individual moral perspectives, the same Kantian criteria and the same logic of normative justification apply to both. Indeed, it would be perverse—in Kantian terms, a violation of the prescriptivity criterion—to argue that reasoning that was better than other reasoning in theory was not better when made the basis for cultural practice.[24]

The Dynamics of Moral Development

Despite the normative similarity of Kohlberg's six stages as individual and cultural stages, the dynamics of moral development are not the dynamics of cultural change: a culture is by no means subject to the same forces as an individual. The dynamics of cultural change are discussed in Chapter 5, and both to prepare for that discussion and to round out the presentation of Kohlberg's theory, we examine here some research findings about how moral development occurs and about other characteristics of the stages.

As noted earlier, people move through the sequence of stages without retrogressing and without skipping any stages. Stage changes occur, if at all, only upward between adjacent stages. Development is not inevitable, and people may "top out" at any stage. On the other hand, people may also continue to progress or may recommence motion after a hiatus.

Moral development occurs slowly. Kohlberg's longitudinal results from U.S. children indicate that the three transitions from Stage 1 to Stage 4 require a total of about eighteen years—from Stage 1 around age eight to Stage 4 around age twenty-six. (See Colby et al., 1983.) Each transition, in other words, takes about six years to accomplish, despite the ready availability of cultural support for each one in the form of children's books, films, school curricula, and the general example of the culture itself.

There appear to be specific "mileposts" in the acquisition of each new stage. A person at a given stage begins the transition at the "ignorance" milepost: in total ignorance of any higher stage, so that higher stage reasoning is either heard as nonsense, misinterpreted as reasoning within the person's own stage, or dismissed as reasoning at some lower, previously superseded stage. (We will refer to reasoning at the person's current stage as "+0 reasoning," at subsequent stages as +1, +2, etc., reasoning, and at previous stages as -1, -2, etc., reasoning.) Thus a Stage 2 child repeats the Golden Rule as "Do unto others as they do unto you," failing entirely to grasp the complexities of the Stage 3 ideal relationship represented in the correct ". . . as you would have them . . ." phrasing (Kohlberg, 1981a:149).

The first evidence that a stage transition is taking place is "awareness," the reasoner's recognition of the possibility that a +1 reasoner is not speaking nonsense; that her own lack of comprehension may be due to ignorance rather than to the other's attempt to be mysterious. The existence of this milepost has apparently not been studied directly, but Kohlberg's (1981:46) remarks on moral leadership seem to contemplate such an initial step. Awareness of another's +1 reasoning does not persuade a reasoner, but it does create a "wait and see" attitude. Lower-stage (and nonsensical) reasoning can be dismissed; reasoning which one does not quite grasp is more unnerving.

The milepost of awareness is followed by that of "preference," when the reasoner comes to prefer +1 reasoning to her own. This phenomenon has been studied by Rest (1973) and forms the basis for his Defining Issues Test (1972). Preference would appear to be closely related to "recognition"—the ability to pick out from several alternatives the argument most like a criterion argument. (See Gavaghan, Arnold, and Gibbs, 1983, and the references cited therein. Rest, 1976, mentions but does not discuss the recognition ability.)

Preference is important for direct persuasion of others, but it is limited in its effect because these others may not be able to repeat the arguments to persuade third parties. That ability, here termed "reproduction," comes next in the transition: when the reasoner is able to rephrase correctly the higher stage's reasoning in her own terms. Such rephrasing is dependent, however, on a model being provided. (See Selman, 1971, for research on reproduction.)

The "reproducer's" necessity for a model vanishes at the milepost of "production." At this point the individual is able autonomously to produce a +1 analysis of a moral problem. Kohlberg's Moral Judgment Interview tests for this milepost. Following Kohlberg, I define production as signaling the consolidation of a new stage; the phrase "+1 reasoning" thus turns to "+0 reasoning" at this milepost.

There is, however, one further milepost—the "teaching" ability, when the individual is able to produce the new stage's reasoning self-consciously and in slow motion. In teaching, justification for the logical processes must go beyond statements like "That's the way it has to be done" or "It feels right," which would be perfectly acceptable at the "production" milepost. This milepost has apparently been neither studied nor discussed, so its role in the transition to a new stage is unknown.

This discussion of stage transitions is speculative to some extent and clearly needs empirical study. The particular order in which the abilities appear has not been studied (but see Rest, 1976:201-202), and although the order given above seems logically inevitable, empirical research is clearly needed. Two of the mileposts, awareness and teaching, have not been studied at all, and I describe them simply to stimulate research. Empirical research is also needed to determine whether a stage transition can halt at one of the mileposts (and if so, which ones) and whether, having reached a certain milepost (and if so, which one), the transition will inevitably complete itself.

We now turn from stage transitions to look at related

developmental sequences. As shown in the works of Piaget and his many followers, the genetic-epistemological model of cognitive development applies to many domains of cognition. Piaget, alone or with coworkers, studied the child's conceptions not only of morality but also of physical causality, number, physical quantity, time, and their many subconcepts and related concepts. In recent years Piagetian scholars have studied a variety of aspects of what is called "social cognition": role-taking, personal identity, empathy, "Ideals of the Good Life," and so on.[25]

Despite the content differences among these many areas of cognition, they share a common sequence of abstract structures. In each cognitive domain he studied, Piaget pointed to the same sequence of developmental stages: sensory-motor operations, pre-operational thought, concrete-operational thought, and formal-operational thought. Since each abstract cognitive structure applies to many specific content domains, the structures create as many parallel developmental sequences as there are domains.

The many parallel sequences do not develop synchronously, however: there is a systematic order in which people apply a given stage to the different content areas. Piaget calls this phenomenon "horizontal decalage," and it is seen in the acquisition of different forms of conservation (Flavell, 1963), in the acquisition prior to moral development of necessary logical skills (DeVries and Kohlberg, 1977; Kuhn et al., 1977) and role-taking skills (Selman, 1971; Selman and Damon, 1975), and in the uneven rates of moral development in different areas. (See Gilligan et al., 1971, on sexual dilemmas. See Lieberman, 1972, for a comparison of all areas tested by Kohlberg.) It appears to arise from differential "resistances" of the content domains to the given structure—the relative difficulty of applying a certain stage's cognitive schema to a specific area of reality. The source of the difficulty may be social in nature; for example, the society may teach Stage X reasoning first in one specific area and only later, or not at all, in others. The source may also be purely physical; for example, children generally recognize that stretching a rubber band leaves its weight unchanged earlier than they recognize that rolling out a clay ball leaves its weight unchanged. The rubber band snaps back "by itself," so to speak, whereas the clay ball must be forced into its various shapes. Though the cognitive relationship of reversibility is the same in both cases, it is more readily seen in one content area than in the other.[26]

Kohlberg and his associates have shown that moral reasoning occurs late in the horizontal decalage order. It is preceded by role-taking (Selman, 1971) and by concepts of space and matter (Colby, 1976; Walker, 1980). Indeed, judging from the fact that no content area has been found to occur later than moral reasoning, the latter would seem to be the most difficult of all areas.

Despite the known existence of horizontal decalage, cognitive development does not proceed independently in different areas. In moral reasoning, for example, Kohlberg claims that the variation in the different areas tapped by his instrument is less than one stage (Colby et al., 1983). One would expect that more varied cognitive material would show more varied stages, of course. Nevertheless, cognitive development research finds that acquisition of a given stage propagates across the individual's cognitive space, transforming that space's structure as it goes. Thus at the individual level we find horizontal decalage between cognitive areas, but not complete independence of development.

In addition to what Kohlberg, Levine, and Hewer (1984a:30) call the "hard structural" Piagetian theories of development, there are other theories that appear linked to the Piagetian sequence. Such theories are what Kohlberg, Levine, and Hewer (1984a:30) call "soft structural" theories—those of Loevinger (1966); Perry (1970); Fowler (1981); and Maslow (1954). (Maslow's theory is not treated in the above-cited discussion of soft structural theories.) Kohlberg, Levine, and Hewer (1984a) note that such theories share many Piagetian assumptions about development and loosely fit the Piagetian criteria for (hard) structural stage theories. (See also the discussion in Habermas, 1979b.) Despite the philosophical and theoretical differences between hard and soft structural theories, their developmental sequences would seem to parallel one another. I mention the possible parallelism because research in these other theories may prove relevant to the present theory, which is based on Kohlberg's work. Soft structural theories cannot provide a basis for a theory of development, however, because they are not normatively grounded.[27]

Notes

1. This is the basic question for deontological moralities, at least, which are concerned with duty and obligation. It is not as basic (but may have some relevance nonetheless) for teleological moralities, which justify action based on the pursuit of ultimate moral ends.

2. Habermas (1979a, 1979b) and McCarthy (1979) discuss the necessary connection between ways of relating and ethical questions. Kohlberg (1981a) carefully refutes cultural relativists' and moral relativists' attempts to disconnect ways of relating from ethical questions.

3. Flavell (1968); Selman (1971); Piaget (1977); Habermas (1979, esp. 1979b and 1979c); Higgins, Ruble, and Hartup (1983); and Overton (1983) discuss various aspects of the general connection among moral reasoning, role-taking, and social behavior. Berti, Bombi, and Lis (1982) and Berti, Bombi, and De Bene (1986) describe the Piagetian developmental acquisition of economic conceptions about means of production, owners, and profit. Habermas (1975, 1979) has been particularly concerned with the connection among social behavior, moral reasoning and the state's ability to legitimize its rule. See Piaget (1932); Kohlberg (1984a); and Colby et al. (1983) for general discussions of the moral development research tradition. See Kohlberg (1981) and Kohlberg, Levine, and Hewer (1984a) for a discussion of the claims presented here. Attacks on these claims can be found in Fishkin (1982), Gilligan (1982), Gibbs (1977), and other authors cited in Kohlberg, Levine & Hewer (1984b). The latter work contains Kohlberg's replies to those attacks.

The applicability of Piagetian cognitive-developmental sequences to diverse fields of social cognition provides another justification for this work's refusal to restrict its analysis to a narrowly construed "political development."

In view of the arguments surrounding Kohlberg's work, I will clarify its role in this book. First, the present analytic framework requires only that some sequence of stages satisfy the five claims given in the text below. Critics like Gilligan (1982) and Gibbs (1977) attack only Kohlberg's particular sequence, conceding that some such sequence must exist. That is all this work requires. (Some critics, like Geertz, 1984, deny the possibility of any such sequence.) Second, I must say in all fairness that I have examined Kohlberg's concepts, methods, and results carefully, and while I interpret the sequence slightly differently from Kohlberg, as shown in this chapter, I have no quarrel with the stage definitions themselves.

4. Specific definitions of the stages are lengthy and are not required for the purposes of this book. The interested reader should consult Kohlberg (1984) or Colby and Kohlberg (forthcoming). The six stages are termed Stage 1, Stage 2...Stage 6. Cognitive stages below

Stage 1 differentiate morality so little from other concepts that they are not of much theoretical or (given their rarity in the adult population) practical interest, and Stage 6 does not occur with sufficient frequency to allow an empirical test of Kohlberg's philosophical argument for its developmental location or even its existence. There is a transitional period, possibly a stage, of extreme philosophical relativism between Stages 4 and 5—Stage 4 1/2. Colby and Kohlberg (forthcoming) present Kohlberg's method of stage scoring, and Colby et al. (1983) present data on scoring reliability.

5. The stages of moral reasoning are most emphatically not evaluations of people's moral worth. A person employing Stage 1 reasoning is no less and no more worthy of having her claims to moral treatment respected than a person employing the fabled Stage 6 reasoning. Just as philosophers critique one another's positions as being ambiguous and having unfortunate implications, without thereby condemning one another as evil people, so does Kohlberg's sequence of stages systematize and abstract the critiques in terms of reasoning structures, without thereby condemning the various reasoners (Kohlberg, 1981: esp. Parts 1 and 2).

6. Different societies have different mixtures of stages. Research suggests that moral reasoners in pre-literate societies rarely or never develop beyond Stage 3. Recall note 5's caution: while we may evaluate moral reasoning as more or less adequate, we cannot judge the reasoners themselves as good or bad people, and thus even less can we extend evaluation to entire collections of reasoners.

7. Kohlberg, Levine, and Hewer (1984a) discuss the structure-content distinction. Cross-cultural studies of reasoning obviously will have many methodological difficulties, but such difficulties alone do not constitute theoretical impossibilities. Geertz (1984) denies the possibility of any cross-culturally valid analytic scheme but offers no support for his claim. Indeed, it is difficult to see how one could ever prove the impossibility of such a framework. Kohlberg (1981a) argues this in detail.

8. Colby and Kohlberg (forthcoming). Other tests of moral reasoning make use of the facts that people at a given stage (a) prefer and (b) can recapitulate arguments at that level. Preference forms the basis for Rest's (1972) test of moral judgment. Turiel (1966) and Selman (1971) explore the ability of people to recapitulate moral reasoning at different stages.

9. Even here it is anticipated by McClelland's (1976) and Aronoff's (1967, 1970) theme analyses. Radding's (1978, 1979, and 1985) arguments are directly cognitive-structural.

10. The following discussion owes much to Flavell (1963).

11. This discussion is not given for Stage 1, because its prior stage is not described.

12. For example, in order to encourage the current attempts at

cultural innovation, Phyllis Rose (1983) deliberately explores a variety of Victorian solutions to the problems of marriage.

13. This discussion is not given for Stage 6, which would not be the final stage if moral problems remained. Kohlberg (1981b) argues Stage 6's validity.

14. Note that this description is from the subordinate's point of view. Obviously "big people" can relate to others at Stage 1 as well.

15. Stage 1 reasoning is rare in adult populations, so this view of its nature is probably more hostile than it would be "naturally." Adult Stage 1 reasoners find it difficult to interact easily in a society whose interpersonal forms are largely beyond their comprehension. The unthinking obedience to authorities, or the correlative demand for the unthinking obedience of others, characterizes society's Eichmanns and criminals. It also seems obvious that only severe forms of early abuse and neglect, emotional or physical, could halt moral development in a society drenched in more developed reasoning. The picture of Stage 1 interpersonal relations we gain from Stage 1 adults is therefore distorted by these reasoners' early difficulties and later conflicts with a bafflingly complex world.

16. Bloch (1961:Chapter 4 and pp. 337ff) discusses corvee labor and prebend.

17. That is, imbalances relative to what could occur in a Stage 2 direct exchange.

18. There are many specific forms of godparenting even within the cultures mentioned. The point is that at least some of these forms embody Stage 3 obligations. I am indebted to José Garcia for information on *compadrazgo*'s variations in Latin America. (See Montes, 1979.)

19. "One major problem" refers to the internal contradictions of Stage 3, not to Stage 3 attempts to deal with Stages 1 and 2, where "turning the other cheek" would not be a reciprocal relationship.

20. Kohlberg (1984b:630) notes that Stage 3 reasoners express universalizability when they say "All people should obey the law because without laws immoral people would cause chaos," which sounds like the Stage 4 argument just given. But the contradiction is only apparent: "chaos" is employed in two different senses. In the Stage 4 sense, chaos refers to the essential conflict between Stage 3 obligations: Heinz can be "nice" to his wife or "nice" to the druggist, but he can't be "nice" to both. In the Stage 3 sense, chaos refers to a breakdown of mutuality entirely, so that Heinz will start "looking out for number one."

21. This law was recognized by general Theban opinion, according to Haemon.

22. Gilligan (1982) points out this dichotomy. She argues that it appears in Kohlberg's work, but I believe Stage 6 implicitly connects the two languages in its refusal to distinguish moral claims of self and

other. Rawls's Original Position, for example, originates in a basic attitude of care and responsibility for others. (Kohlberg, Levine, and Hewer, 1984b:338-370, respond to Gilligan's arguments.)

23. For further discussion of these normative claims, see Kohlberg (1981a, 1981b), and Kohlberg, Levine, and Hewer (1984a). The nature of the duality of the psychological and philosophical claims is discussed in the exchange between Habermas (1983) and Kohlberg, Levine, and Hewer (1984b). Briefly, empirical study of the stages tests the adequacy of the philosophical conceptions in a negative way: empirical falsification of the sequence demonstrates problems with the philosophical framework, but empirical support of the sequence cannot go on to support its philosophical claim of moral adequacy. (This interaction is clearly seen in Kohlberg's response to early findings of apparent regression, such as those reported in Kohlberg and Kramer, 1969.) On the other hand, a philosophical position is required to justify a test instrument in the first place. The analyst can easily create an instrument but cannot assert that it measures morality without some philosophical position of what morality is. Kohlberg's arguments against Hartshorne and May's early work on morality focus largely on the inadequate conception of the moral domain implied by their assessment methods.

24. Gilligan and Murphy (1979) argue that real moral dilemmas may call forth different moral reasoning than hypothetical dilemmas. Assuming this is true, this does not negate the criterion of prescriptivity (indeed, is an appeal to it), but instead implies that Kohlberg's methods may be flawed. (Gilligan, 1982, also suggests this.) As mentioned in note 3, however, the present analytic framework's validity does not rest on any particular sequence of stages—the ones given above can be taken as merely illustrative—but only on the existence of some sequence of stages, the existence of which Gilligan does not dispute. (See also the discussion in Kohlberg, Levine, and Hewer, 1984b.)

25. Overton (ed) (1983) contains several articles and numerous references in the area of social cognition. See also Higgins, Ruble, and Hartup (1983). "Ideals of the Good Life" are studied by Armon (1984).

26. The decalage may well differ from culture to culture, however, particularly in the domains of social cognition. The existence of decalages is inherent in the Piagetian perspective, but (in contradistinction to the ordering of the structural stages themselves) the ordering of the decalages is not.

27. Examples of development research or analytic frameworks founded on such "soft structural" stages include Davies (1977, 1986); Aronoff (1967); Eckstein (1982); and Park (1984).

FOUR

The Hierarchy of Forms of Political Culture

Structure, Morality, Culture, and Institutions

Chapter 3 led our attention toward abstract considerations. It started with ways of relating, argued that moral reasoning is constituted in the ways of relating, and finally discussed moral reasoning development as one aspect of the more general development of abstract cognitive structures. Although this abstraction is useful for presenting and clarifying the Piagetian perspective on moral development, political development is not, after all, a development of abstract intellectual structures but the development of concrete social arrangements. Recall that these abstract structures present themselves to us as ways of relating that are of potential use in the social world.

The ways of relating contemplated by the moral reasoning stages are only ideals or potentials, however, until they become the basis of actual relationships and, more broadly, actual social arrangements. A social actor can only carry them out in concrete social arrangements if she has like-minded and cooperative others. The term we use for this mutual use of a way of relating is "public commonness," and if a given way of relating is publicly common, the people sharing it form a culture.

Each member of the culture relates to other members in the cultural way of relating. These relationships within the culture create institutions through two mechanisms. First, institutions can arise from simple replication of individual pair-relationships. For example, a hierarchy can arise as the replication downward of individual dominance-submission relations. Replication is the sole source of social institutions at Stages 1 to 3, since they have no vision of social orderings beyond dyads. Second, institutions can arise from the actors' shared determination to interact within a specific, larger, institutional framework. An institution is, after all, nothing more than a group of people acting intentionally within its framework.

Chapter 3 asked what individual relationships or ways of relating were characteristic of each moral reasoning stage. This chapter asks what social forms beyond individual relationships—that is, what institutions—can social actors create when limited to a given stage's ways of relating. Table 3 summarizes the following discussion.

In order to determine the ideal-typical institutions associated with each stage, this chapter's analysis presumes a culture exists. This assumption does not mean any loss of generality for this work's overall analytic framework, however, since no claim is made that any specific society has a culture.

Table 3. Speculative Classification of Social Forms

Interpersonal Relations/ Forms of Influence	Associated Social Institutions
1 Domination; physical compulsion; threats; seizure by force; extortion	Pecking order; slavery; prison and other total institutions
2 Barter and trading; deterrence by revenge; bribery; corvee labor; prebend; curses; feudal fealty and vassalage	Early feudal system; exchange patronage systems; tax farming; hostages
3 Friendship; *compadrazgo*; romantic or courtly love	Medieval towns; social patronage or client system; late-medieval aristocracy; estates *(Staende)*; dualistic *Staendestaat*; corporatism
4 Mutual support of moral system	Modern army; bureaucracy; fascism; tyranny of majority rule; absolutism
5 Mutual respect; rational debate, fair competition, and scientific testing	Democracies protecting civil rights and liberties; due process; capitalist market economies; "normal science"
6 *Satyagraha; agape*; undistorted communicative action; mutual care	[none currently known]

(This is a matter for empirical determination in each case.) Sub-cultures, cultural ignorance, and dissent obviously create certain social dynamics (e.g., repression, conflict, compromise, development), but dynamics will not concern us until the next chapter.

Six Stages of Institutions and Other Behavioral Regularities

Stage 1 possesses few and very simple ways of relating. The institutions built up from these relationships are accordingly very limited, restricted to pecking-order hierarchies and slavery. Even such an "institution" as an extortion racket involves at heart no more than one person threatening another; little organization is involved. The organization emerging from Stage 1 is the result of immediate responses, not of any social vision.

Do any Stage 1 institutions currently exist, and have they existed in the past? Bullying and extortion rackets still exist among children and to some extent among adults, and slavery still exists in isolated areas of the world. Maximum-security prisons may contain a Stage 1 culture. Radding (personal communication) has speculated that Nazism was based on a Stage 1 worship of force.[1]

The social forms built up from Stage 2 relationships are more varied than Stage 1 forms, but still operate on the narrow bases of positive exchange (bribery) and negative exchange (revenge). For example, the Roman, Byzantine, and other empires were organized on the "venal control" or "tax farming" system (Frey, 1971), which relied only on Stage 2 relationships. Governors related to the emperor on a positive exchange basis, giving the emperor both protection from outlying barbarians and an annual tribute levied on the subject population, while receiving both military support and the right to all taxes collected beyond the emperor's tribute. The governor's loyalty was additionally ensured by the negative exchange practice of keeping hostages: the governor's family would remain in the Imperial capital or even in the emperor's household and thus could be punished for any misdeeds of the governor.[2] This straightforward Stage 2 relationship between emperor and governor was duplicated at lower levels: between the governor and his subgovernors; between each subgovernor and his district superintendents; between each district superintendent and the district's village headmen; and between each village headman and the heads of the village families.

Note that no vision of the overall tax farming system is required by its participants: what appears to be a complex totality is composed simply of nested, individual, Stage 2 relationships. This is a good example of how the replication process can create broad social forms out of individual relationships.

Stage 2 institutions have existed in many areas and eras, not just in empires. The early feudal ages were characterized by Stage 2 organization; feudal lords exchanged protection for rent and service from their vassals.[3] Feuds, though the term apparently arises from a different word than feudal, also are based on a Stage 2 relationship of systematic, alternating revenge. Feuds may not ordinarily be considered social institutions, but they certainly represent regularly occurring behavior motivated by a publicly common way of relating, and so accordingly deserve to be termed a "social form." Bloch (1961: Chapter 9, Section 2) discussed the "vendetta," which had some legal/social sanction as late as the thirteenth century. It should be no surprise that Stage 2 feudal society should include such a social form. Currently, political scientists study Stage 2 institutions in terms of "clientelism," a concept applicable to institutions worldwide. The research collections of Schmidt et al. (1977) and of Eisenstadt and Lemarchand (1981) include studies of clientelism in societies both Western and non-Western, developing and developed, urban and rural. The pervasiveness of clientelism would appear to arise from the simplicity of its underlying cognitive structure.

Although Stage 2 institutions obviously exist around the world, social scientists appear to be preoccupied with them to the point that Stage 3 ties are misread as thin disguises for selfish interests. Lande (1977:507-508), for example, writes his theory of dyadic relationships exclusively in Stage 2 terms: "Dyadic relationships, being systems of exchange or barter, must be between individuals who are unalike. . . . [One partner] is not likely to be asked to interest himself in the [other's] trade as a whole. . . . The interests that unite the leader and his followers are particular rather than categorical: the purpose is not the attainment of a common general objective

but the advancement of the leader's and his followers' comple-
mentary private interests." Hall's (1977) theoretical discussion
of the patron-client relationship follows similar lines. Such
formulations miss Stage 3 institutional forms (e.g., of patron-
client relations), not by ignoring them but, more perniciously, by
reading them as Stage 2. The fact that Stage 3 reasoners come
to their decisions in structurally more complex ways than Stage
2 reasoners is ignored in the retrospective cynicism of social-
scientific analysis. Rawls (1971) has pointed out that utilitarianism can always read retrospectively any principled moral
decision as self-interest. As Radding (1979) argues in a similar
context, such analyses dismiss the plainly stated reasons actors
advance for their actions.

Stage 3 institutions are characterized by the grouping of
people, each of whom maintains mutual ties with the other
members. Several excellent examples were created in medieval
France, starting around the twelfth century: cities, towns, and
communes; the aristocracy; the estates (*Staende*); and the dual-
istic system (*Staendestaat*) by which Rule was created through
the cooperation of the *Staende* and the ruler. Each of these
institutions was created from the same Stage 3 cooperation
among elements. Pirenne (1952:180-181) explains how towns,
for example, were integrated: "The burghers formed a corps, a
universitas, a *communitas*, a *communio*, all the members of
which, conjointly answerable to one another, constituted in
inseparable parts . . . the city of the Middle Ages did not con-
sist in a simple collection of individuals; it was itself an
individual, but a collective individual, a legal person." Poggi
(1978:37-38) notes that this collective creation differed from
earlier institutions based on dyadic ties of feudal vassalage.
Each town formed a collective identity out of the individual
equality of its citizens, and the old, Stage 2 relationship of
feudal vassalage was banished in the towns: both Pirenne
(1952:193) and Poggi (1978:40) note the German proverb
"*Stadtluft macht frei*" (city air emancipates). This joining
together of equals is characteristic of other late-medieval
institutions. The landed aristocracy joined with the poorer
knights in a solidarity of chivalry: "The consciousness of class
which gradually caused the French aristocracy to become a
homogeneous group was thus crystallized around the knightly
ideal, its ethic and the virtues of wisdom and loyalty" (Duby,
1977:180). This new association among the aristocracy was also

made among towns. These associations were the estates (*Staende*)—again, a collective creation of formally equal and individually weak participants. The *Staende*, in turn, cooperated with the territory's ruler to create Rule. Rule was not exercised directly by the ruler as a right, but rather came from the cooperative association. This concept, often termed dualism, "suggests that the territorial ruler and the Staende make up the polity jointly, but as separate and mutually acknowledged political centers. Both constitute it, through their mutual agreement; but even during the agreement's duration they remain distinct, each exercising powers of its own, and differing in this from the 'organs' of the mature, 'unitary' modern state" (Poggi, 1978:48).

The above passage leads us directly into the consideration of Stage 4 institutions, where the abstract principle of Rule is recognized as a prerequisite of social organization itself, not as a byproduct of mutual, bilateral agreement.[4] As Poggi (1978:68) puts it: "In the absolutist state the political process is no longer structured primarily by the continuous, legitimate tension and collaboration between two independent centers of rule, the ruler and the Staende; it develops around and from the former only." Instead of being one of the centers of power whose "interpersonal" cooperation constituted a Stage 3 ideal relationship, the ruler is now the expression of Rule itself. (See Poggi, 1978:Chapter 4.)

Institutions built up from Stage 4 relationships are accordingly absolutistic in character: the modern army, bureaucracies (prior to Weberian rationality), absolute monarchies, fascist government, governments without civil liberties (i.e., subject to the domination of one group—"the tyranny of the majority"), and religions claiming absolute moral authority. Sacred custom, sacred law, sacred procedures, sacred religion—whatever the sacred system is, it constitutes a Stage 4 society. In Almond and Verba's (1963) terms, such societies are "subject" political cultures. Citizens are aware of and orient to the overarching moral authority represented by the state, but have no sense that they themselves create and can alter that authority. Stage 4 conceptualizes society as a totality, and this permits great variability in institutional forms. As long as the institution establishes consistent role requirements, public support (ideally) will follow.

In Europe, the transition to Stage 4 institutions can be seen in the reign of France's Louis XIV (1643-1715). Louis replaced the provincial feudal nobility with his own administrators and, by drawing the nobility to his court in Paris, made himself the arbiter of their fortunes. He thus replaced the Stage 3 feudal ties represented by the system of estates with Stage 4 direction from his single, overarching authority.[5]

Stage 5 relationships can be found in at least three institutions: constitutional democracy, as conceptualized by John Locke and Thomas Jefferson; capitalist market economy, as conceptualized by Adam Smith and his non-Marxian successors; and science, as conceptualized by Karl Popper. Note that these three institutions are ideal-typical; no particular society, including the United States, need have institutions structured at this level.

Locke and Jefferson's theory of constitutional democracy presumes attitudes of mutual respect among citizens; such respect makes possible the recognition of rights existing prior to a social contract—the "inalienable rights" of the Declaration of Independence. Such rights are inalienable because they are inherent in the preexisting moral relationship of mutual respect. The democratic (or representative) form of government reflects the relationship of mutual respect. In addition, the procedures for creating, administering, and adjudicating public law reflect the relationship of rational debate. The right of free speech and press and the right to petition Congress stem from the necessity of gathering all relevant information before a decision. Stage 5 rules of procedure are designed (or at least are evaluated in terms of our desire) to allow all sides to be heard. Due process in both execution and adjudication of laws reflects a desire to ensure that all interests have an opportunity to be heard.

The capitalist market economy, as seen by Adam Smith, also has these characteristics of mutual respect and rational debate. Mutual respect makes possible the basic agreements of the market system: the agreement upon everyone's right to buy and sell freely; the agreement upon an abstract medium of exchange; the agreement upon an impartial regulatory body of sufficient strength to preserve the conditions of free trade. What the relationship of rational debate is to constitutional democracy, the relationship of fair competition is to market economies. Fair competition allows all factors to be taken into account in a decision to buy or sell: the buyer or seller, like the rational debater, is provided with the entire range of alternatives to choose from.

Science resembles a free market system in that the "stock" (in the colloquial sense) of a theory rises or falls according to whether scientists "buy" it. Scientists start from a position of mutual respect—a recognition that their colleagues hold initially different beliefs and yet all seek scientific truth. This recognition enables scientists to work cooperatively toward their mutual goal, even though they may appear to be competing with one another for the adoption of their own theories.[6] The procedures of scientific testing implement that cooperative effort. Theories must be tested against real-world evidence through reproducible tests of hypotheses. The process is rational, in that hypotheses derived from "true" theories will be repeatedly confirmed and hypotheses of the other sort will at some time be disconfirmed. The criterion employed—that theory be able to predict empirical consequences—is acceptable to all concerned, and it is open enough to allow all relevant information to be gathered before a decision is made on a theory's validity.[7]

We will not speculate here about what institutions would reflect Stage 6 relationships. As noted earlier, Kohlberg has not encountered such reasoning with sufficient frequency to prove empirically that it lies beyond Stage 5. Social institutions are invented when a group of people can relate to one another in the same way; accordingly, the development of Stage 6 institutions must await a larger concentration of Stage 6 reasoners. (Rawls, 1971:Section 43, suggests possible governmental arrangements of the Just Society. The social forms discussed by Jackins, 1987, are also of interest in this connection.)

Structure and Content

The previous discussion applies Kohlberg's micro-level theory of cognitive structure to a macro-level theory of institutional content. Kohlberg can justify his theory as nonethnocentric because of its content neutrality. Does the emphasis on institutional content make our macro-level theory ethnocentric?

Genetic epistemology is not a scientistic denigration of foreign ways of thought but rather a culture-free theory of structural development. Consider a Stage 2 reasoner thinking through the question of whether a husband should steal a drug that could save his wife's life. Within the Stage 2 reasoning structure, questions of right or wrong depend on decisions of what is good or bad for the reasoner. Thus a common Stage 2 answer is that stealing the drug would be wrong because you might get caught and put in jail. Kohlberg (1981a:115) reports the opposite answer given by a Stage 2 Taiwanese village youth to a similar story: "He should steal the food for his wife, because if she dies he'll have to pay for her funeral and that costs a lot." Though the two answers differ in their content (both in the decision made and in the considerations adduced for that decision), the answers were the same in the structure of the reasoning used. In both cases morality is judgment from only a single perspective; other people do not enter into the decision except insofar as they can help or hurt one. This example illustrates that the structure of moral reasoning can be identified and studied independently of either cultural or individual variations in content.

Granted, cultural bias can and undoubtedly does creep into the actual coding of the research instruments. For example, it may be, as Gilligan (1982) argues, that women are scored too low by Kohlberg's scoring manual. Interviewers and coders eventually come to rest believing they understand the cognitive structures supporting their respondents' use of such terms as "love," "honor," etc. If one group of people has a more complex meaning for these terms than another, then one group or the other will be misscored unless the difference in meanings is recognized and explored.

However, this does not mean that the genetic epistemological paradigm itself is biased; it only shows that specific means of identifying cognitive structures can be in error. Researchers' ability to test alternative scoring methods by empirical study means that the methods are not trapped in bias, even if they contain it.[8]

This chapter's conception of political development uses specific institutions to exemplify different developmental stages, but the stages are defined in terms of their organizing structures. Being based on structure rather than content, this conception of political development is culture-free. All cultures can be placed within the stage sequence, and any given structural stage can describe many different institutions from different cultural traditions. Furthermore, development does not require a culture to become like any more-developed culture, but instead requires that each culture resolve the structural ambiguities of its current stage in its own fashion. Even though there is a culturally universal sequence of organizing structures, there is no universal sequence of specific social forms.

Notes

1. A few notes of clarification are required here. (a) Recall from the discussion in Chapter 3 that adult Stage 1 reasoners are likely to have special problems interacting with more developed reasoners and are likely to have remained at their reasoning levels because of unique difficulties in their upbringing. The social behavior flowing from Stage 1 reasoning accordingly cannot be judged by the behavior of adult Stage 1 reasoners. Stage 1 children do not run around as slavers, extortioners, and bullies. On the other hand, the absence of such behavior may stem from the higher stage reasoning of the adult authorities who define so much of the moral world for them. (This is the thesis of *Lord of the Flies*.) We cannot, therefore, discuss "natural" Stage 1 social behavior with any confidence. ("Natural" means societies that have evolved organically, in contradistinction to artificially constructed societies like prisons.)

(b) I have encountered a surprising amount of skepticism among other moral development researchers that a Stage 1 society exists or ever could have existed. They argue that Stage 1 reasoning is too simple, too unmoral to create a society at all. Such a position, however, seems inconsistent with the basic perspective of genetic epistemology. Knowledge is constructed, stage by stage, and therefore somewhere between John Rawls and the primeval ooze there must have been a time when Stage 1 was the pinnacle of human (prehuman?) intellectual achievement. Stage 1 societies therefore must have existed in the (possibly very distant) past.

(c) Could recent times have seen a "natural" Stage 1 society? Again, despite my colleagues' skepticism, I think such a society is quite possible, although Western society's penetration of even the remotest regions constantly lessens this possibility. My colleagues' skepticism arises, I think, from a correct reluctance to equate our cultural background with a maximum security prison. Recognition that the latter is distorted by its situation within our present, far different society should alter their skepticism.

2. Note that punishment of miscreants' families occurs in many early legal systems. See Bloch (1961) on the medieval European vendetta, and Hobhouse (1906:Chapter 3) for examples from many other cultures.

3. See Bloch (1961) and Poggi (1978) for a discussion of the specifics of feudal relationships. Hear Poggi's (1978:24-25) description of the hierarchical extension of Stage 2 feudal relations: "Historically,

however, the elaboration of the lord-vassal relationship mostly advanced *downward*. Typically, a territorial ruler, finding it impossible to operate a system of rule constituted of impersonal, official roles, sought to bridge the gap between himself and the ultimate objects of rule—the populace—-by relying primarily on his retinue of trusted warriors. To this end, he endowed them with fiefs from the landed domain under his charge . . . ; but his immediate vassals often carved from their own fiefs smaller ones for the members of *their* retinues."

4. Wolin (1960) makes this point in his discussion of Hobbes.

5. See Deutsch, Dominguez, and Heclo (1981:189-191). Thomas Wright (1984) presents a study of the first Ibañez administration in Chile that shows striking parallels between Ibañez's and Louis XIV's methods.

6. Just as free-market theory sees entrepreneurs cooperatively benefiting society through their selfish competition.

7. Thomas Kuhn (1970a, 1970b) calls this form of science "normal science."

8. Recall the discussion in Chapter 3:note 23, about the mutual checks provided by the theoretical-philosophical and empirical-psychological aspects of moral development research.

FIVE

Developmental Dynamics

We have discussed an ordering of social forms, and the conception of political development appears to have overcome the five "fundamental theoretical challenges" raised in Chapter 1. But the discussion to this point has been fairly static. We know from earlier research how individuals move from stage to stage, but we have not yet asked how cultures might move.

In particular, we would like to address five general issues of political development's dynamics:

1. (Unilinearity) Is there a single developmental path, or are there alternate paths?
2. (Inevitability) What drives development? In particular, what initiates it? Is it historically inevitable? In particular, what is the role of human agency in development? Cyclical theories of history, such as those of Aristotle, Polybius, or Spengler, see no possibility of long-term development. "Spiral" theories of history, such as those of Vico or Toynbee, assert that progress is inevitable despite repeated short-term setbacks. Other theorists, e.g., Hobhouse and Marx, see history as an inevitable, fairly steady progression.
3. (Monotonicity) Is retrogression possible or, as Pye (1978:viii) asserts, is there a "ratchet effect" in development? Can historical cycles occur? Is stasis possible, either brief or long?
4. (Synchrony) Do all elements of society develop equally and simultaneously throughout a society or, as Chilcote (1981:277) and Althusser (1970:Chapter 4) mention, is

79

asynchronous development possible? In Piagetian terms, are there decalages of development between different areas of society?

5. (Continuity) Does development occur in crises and discontinuous changes, as argued in Binder et al. (1971), or does it occur in small, steady increments? Can stages be skipped?

Fortunately, the broad outline of answers to these questions is implicit in the logic of our analytic framework. The major dynamics of development flow from two sources in the conception of development: the dynamics of moral reasoning development and the dynamics of establishing, maintaining, and altering the public commonness of a way of relating.[1] The answers thus indicated require empirical support, and the necessary research will certainly fill in the details with midrange theories and the like, but the broad outlines of the answers seem already implicit.

The issue of unilinearity was dealt with tangentially at the end of the previous chapter. Development is unilinear in the sense that it is always measured along the same sequence of structural stages. It is multilinear in its cultural content, however, since different cultures develop with different institutions. We must distinguish carefully between these two aspects of political development, just as we do for individual development. Taking cognizance only of structures, all development looks the same; taking cognizance of both structure and content, cultures can develop differently. This book is primarily concerned with the unilinear development of structures, but it fully recognizes that each culture has its own institutions, environment, and heritage.

Before we can address the issues of inevitability, monotonicity, synchrony, and continuity, however, we must examine more closely how development occurs. Development of a higher-stage culture requires two changes to occur: the emergence of a new stage of reasoning in the form of ideal ways of relating and their associated institutions, and the realization of these ways of relating—that is, the establishment of their public commonness. These changes have different dynamics. Cognitive growth, manifested in new ways of relating and institutional forms, occurs as an intellectual resolution of cognitive ambiguities felt in the previous stage. Public commonness, on the other hand, requires access to political power sufficient to teach and implement the new ways of relating and institutional forms. In addition, the interaction of these two sets of dynamics creates a further set of dynamics.

This chapter first sets forth specific major forces associated with each set of dynamics. Following this presentation of dynamic forces, we will be able to address definitively the issues raised above.

Cognitive Development: Cognitive Ambiguity

Short of Stage 6, every moral reasoning structure is ambiguous, meaning that application of the same reasoning to different perspectives can yield different conclusions. Stage 3 reasoning, for example, leaves Heinz undecided whether to cast his sympathies with his wife or the druggist. Stage 4 reasoning leaves him uncertain whether to be guided by legal injunctions not to steal or traditional/religious injunctions to care for people in need. Such ambiguities are the engine that powers cognitive development: increasing awareness of both perspectives induces the reasoner to attempt to coordinate them. The structure coordinating them is the next-higher stage. (See Habermas, 1979c:79; Turiel, 1966, 1974, and 1977; and Walker, 1980, 1983.)

These ambiguities within individuals' reasoning can also appear, writ large, in a society. If public issues are susceptible to two lines of reasoning at the same stage, citizens at that stage will find themselves divided and in conflict. The civil disobedience and official brutality during the civil rights movement, for example, could be viewed in Stage 4 terms either as legitimately firm official responses to blacks' repeated, deliberate violations of law and social convention, or as unmannerly reactions to blacks' politely firm demands for ordinary, courteous treatment. This ambiguity of response split the United States (and the South itself), creating a public debate that revealed, in effect, the inadequacy of both opposing Stage 4 positions. The public debate made salient a variety of resolutions of the conflict in terms of Stage 5 theories of civil rights, even if those resolutions were not always understood and adopted.

Similar ambiguities are involved in creationists' demands that their doctrine be taught in biology courses as a theory competitive with evolution. Creationists see the conflict as a battle over competing opinions about the truth—and many scientists (who ought to know better) take the same view.[2] This conflict cannot be resolved short of Stage 5, where the requirements of empirical falsifiability and hypothetico-deductive logic are understood. Creationism does not generate empirical hypotheses (because God might have done anything) and is not falsifiable (because any arrangement of evidence can be attributed to God's action). Creationist claims may be true, but no one can test them. Creationism is not taught beside evolution because the former is an article of faith while the latter is, even if disputed, a testable theory.[3]

So we see that cognitive development need not occur out of purely individual moral conflicts. These open political conflicts of civil rights and creationism make salient the ambiguity of Stage 4 reasoning and thus allow citizens the opportunity to move from Stage 4 to Stage 5. The cognitive stages structuring cultures manifest their ambiguities in widespread social issues, creating the possibility of widespread cognitive development.

Cognitive Development: +1 Awareness and Preference

As mentioned in Chapter 3, some reasoners at a given stage can (in various limited ways) understand reasoning at the stage above their own. Starting from an initial ignorance of the stage above, reasoners subsequently "are aware of"; "recognize" and "prefer"; and finally "reproduce" +1 reasoning.

Each of these abilities makes reasoners to some degree susceptible to guidance by +1 reasoners. Reproduction underlies the relationship of master and disciple, in which the disciple wishes to acquire the master's facility through hearing and restating the master's reasoning; the ability to reproduce +1 reasoning means that a reasoner can follow and accept a higher-stage analysis, even if she cannot generalize the reasoning to other times and situations. Even if the reasoner is able only to recognize +1 reasoning, she will still recognize it as more adequate and will prefer it, and accordingly the conclusion reached, to other reasoning. And even if the reasoner is only aware that the other person is not speaking nonsense, she will be more cautious about maintaining her own position in the face of reasoning that sounds coherent even while it is not fully understood.

On the other hand, people dismiss reasoning at stages below their own and at stages more than one above their own. Lower stages are understood quite well and dismissed as inadequate, for at least the same reasons that the reasoner earlier found them inadequate. Reasoning two or more stages above is dismissed as gibberish or is understood as ("assimilated to," in Piaget's language) a lower stage. To exercise legitimate authority, therefore, leaders must justify their leadership and decisions with reasons at, or one stage above, the cognitive stage of those they expect to lead.

These observations make especially relevant Katz and Lazarsfeld's theory of the "two-step flow of communications." Since their 1955 study (see also Katz, 1957), social scientists have divided the public into two groups: a relatively large, "inattentive" public and a relatively small, "attentive" public ("opinion leaders"). The inattentive public does not understand or else pays no attention to public affairs, but instead relies on members of the attentive public for explanation of and guidance about issues. To the inattentive public the mass media project a rudimentary image but little depth or detail. Opinion leaders, on the other hand, attend closely to public affairs, both through a variety of media and through personal involvement. The two-step flow of communications means that leaders need to lead only the attentive public, for it will in turn lead the inattentive public. Leaders are thereby relieved from justifying their policies in terms understood by all: the attentive public's support will be sufficient.

This pattern of communications means that leaders can reason up to two stages above many of their followers. They must reason no more than one stage above the attentive public, and in turn the attentive public, if its members wish to remain opinion leaders, must reason no more than one stage above the inattentive public it leads. The overall effect is to allow leaders legitimately to command a much wider variety of followers than if all leadership depended on direct persuasion.

In this age of mass media, however, leaders are available in increasingly immediate, albeit highly impersonal ways to their followers.[4] To the extent that this direct communication substitutes for the more personal, two-step communication pattern, leaders have to couch their appeals in arguments no more than one stage above the people they wish to persuade. The potential would seem to exist for a consequent degradation of public discourse as rhetorical style comes to substitute for the substance of high-level reasoning.

Other societies undoubtedly have communications patterns other than those discussed above.[5] Whatever patterns are involved, however, legitimate influence cannot jump more than one cognitive stage. Because communication systems govern the degree to which this limitation can be overcome, their study must be an important element of political development research.

Cognitive Development:
Legitimacy, Stability, and Justice

A regime's legitimacy and stability are enhanced if decision-makers reason at or just above the cognitive level of the remainder of society. There are several reasons for this. First, no higher-stage alternatives to rule will arise. Even if the existing political system generates some bad decisions, citizens will not immediately be able to construct a radical cure of that system. Same-stage modifications of the existing political system will have similar structural difficulties and so may not appeal even to dissatisfied citizens.[6] Second, citizens will understand how the system works, supporting the existing regime out of a "better the devil you know" feeling. Finally, citizens will tend to give greater credit to decisions they can understand than those they cannot. People will accept discomforts they judge to be fair. Rulers will be able to persuade many or most citizens of the validity of public policy choices. A steady media campaign with such slogans as "Law Is The Basis Of A Free Society" and "Marriage Ties Take Their Strength From Law" would tend to convince Stage 4 reasoners that Heinz should not steal the drug, even if opposite, equally reasonable points of view exist.

Such leadership also keeps the society just, within the current capacity of its people to envision and maintain a structure of justice. For we must recognize that justice does not arise magically from buildings and statutes; rather, it arises from the ability and willingness of people to relate in the structure of justice contemplated in the institutions. The level of moral reasoning found in a society constrains the institutional forms that its citizens are able and willing to create. Leaders can create institutional models for citizens to fill and learn from, but such models must always be within the grasp of their occupants' reasoning—that is, no more than one stage above.

The previous discussion makes the happy assumption that leaders always reason at stages at or above the led. This need not be the case, of course: many circumstances might place a lower-stage reasoner in charge of or dominant over higher-stage reasoners. This arrangement is termed an inversion.[7]

Societies with many inversions will inevitably experience a legitimacy crisis, as the reasoning of the leaders becomes widely criticized by the led. The leaders, unable to comprehend the objections and alternatives, maintain their illegitimate position with increasingly repressive methods. Repression can mean toleration of criticism without remedial action (Marcuse, 1965), suppression and/or control of communication networks, or the outright silencing of critics by intimidation, exile, imprisonment, or death. Societies with many inversions may survive such a legitimacy crisis, even when it continues for some time. However, such a society is as unstable as a balloon: it holds together, but a small pin-prick can destroy it.

This section's analysis is not a scientistic foundation for a meritocracy of cognitive stage. First, arguments for any social arrangement must focus, as Rawls (1971) shows, on its effects on the worst-off position in society. The previous considerations of who understands what, and whether legitimacy crises occur, are grist for normative analysts' mills but are not normative considerations per se. Second, the discussions assume that both leaders and followers come from the same cultural tradition—that +1 reasoners have resolved the problems still actually experienced by their culture's +0 reasoners. It seems unlikely that a Zulu could use Stage 4 reasoning from that culture to solve problems even of Stage 3 reasoning faced by, say, a local U.S. Chamber of Commerce—and vice-versa. Such a cultural difference is extreme, of course, but the general principle remains at any degree of difference: one can preserve the normative virtue of development only by preserving the cultural continuity between specific problems and their specific, higher-stage resolutions.

In sum, a society's overall moral reasoning level limits the types of legitimate social institutions which that society can maintain. Furthermore, the average cognitive levels of the leaders and the led determine the frequency of inversions in the society and thus the long-term stability and legitimacy of its institutions.

Cognitive Development: Average Cognitive Levels

If cognitive levels are so important in political development, it follows that changes in the overall average of moral reasoning stages will be important sources of social change. This section discusses the social dynamics resulting from a rise or fall of average cognitive level.

We begin by cautioning that the inevitability (or at least nonretrogression) of individual moral reasoning development does not imply any corresponding inevitability of its social average. Other things remaining equal, the social average is perpetuated by the ongoing balance between the death of the oldest, most advanced reasoners and the concurrent development of those remaining alive. It is the fallacy of composition to believe that individual dynamics must have parallel social dynamics.

What can cause overall cognitive advances and declines? New socialization techniques, wide exposure to higher-stage reasoners or institutions, indigenous resolution at a higher stage of the ambiguities of an important social issue—all of these and undoubtedly many other circumstances can cause a society's overall cognitive advance. On the other hand, domination by a foreign conqueror, disease, and systematic suppression of higher-stage reasoners by reactionary forces—these and, again, other circumstances can cause overall cognitive decline.

Our interest is not in the multitude of such causes, however, but rather in the dynamic consequences of cognitive advance and decline. We look first at cognitive advance. The average cognitive advance of a population will certainly imply (and may well arise from) an increased recognition that the old culture has illegitimate, arbitrary, or illogical elements. This will stimulate both an increasing criticism of the old culture and a search for new cultural possibilities. Subgroups will form to experiment with, and ultimately to live out, these new cultural possibilities. Cultural history will be rewritten as expressions of the new subculture, just as women's history and black history are currently being rewritten. From these sources a new culture will arise as the old culture accommodates to the new.

At the same time, the breakdown and refashioning of the old culture will set in motion phenomena of reaction. Because the emerging cultural alternative is more highly developed than the existing culture, it will be misunderstood by many people as they assimilate it, in Piaget's sense, to their existing, less structured cultural understanding. If the new is taken to be the same as the old, the society experiences the politics of opportunism and reform, in which limited immediate concessions are sought and granted in ignorance of (or to prevent) fundamental change. Stage +1 cultural proposals may benefit from the respect of +0 reasoners, but they also suffer from those reasoners' natural reluctance to leap into the unknown. Thus the Equal Rights Amendment benefited from the widespread support for women's rights, but suffered from the fear-mongering campaign waged against it (Mansbridge, 1986).

A good example of the effects of cognitive advance is provided by Radding (1979), who attributes the disappearance of the medieval ordeal to a widespread cognitive advance of the population. He argues that the ordeal resembles in its logic the stage of "immanent justice" described by Piaget (1932), and that the ordeals were only one form of the wider range of rituals by which "the early Middle Ages [attempted] to control the physical world" (Radding, 1979:956). The change to a new sense of the physical world, seen in such diverse areas as poetry, natural philosophy, and the procedures for canonizing saints, suggests a change in the cognitive level of the population. The disappearance of the ordeal can then be seen as one among many cultural concomitants of an overall cognitive advance.

The cognitive decline of a population should, other things remaining equal, cause a retrogression of the culture to lower stages. The population becomes increasingly unable to maintain the original culture. The institutional forms might be followed out of habit,[8] but institutional challenges will not be met by adaptations at the original stage level and children will tend not to be socialized to the original stage level. The old forms might even be idolized, but like all idols they will have no life.

The important concept of institutional "challenges" warrants an example. Consider the institution represented by an ideal-typical bureaucracy. Rules in this bureaucracy have a Stage 4 moral justification: rules must be followed to prevent chaos in the handling of the bureaucracy's work. Suppose, however, that the actual bureaucrats were all at lower stages. As Danet (1971) has shown, a bureaucracy's clients use a variety of arguments—moral arguments, in fact. (Although the Stage 1 threats, Stage 2 bribes and, to a lesser extent, Stage 3 appeals to friendship no longer seem moral to us, Kohlberg's work has amply shown that these are the forms of morality characteristic of these levels.) How is a bureaucrat to reply to these arguments? A Stage 4 bureaucrat will of course have no trouble recognizing the inadequacy of these appeals. Even if the threats or bribes are effective, the bureaucracy at least has a preliminary defense against them in its bureaucratic recognition of them as wrong. But suppose that a bureaucrat is at a lower Stage than 4—say, Stage 3. The bureaucrat might dimly feel that the client's appeals in terms of friendship or personal ties are wrong, but Stage 3 counter-arguments give no clear support, as seen in this exchange:

> *Client:* Why don't you just set aside those requirements? After all, I am a friend and neighbor of yours.
> *Bureaucrat:* If I did that I'd disappoint my boss, who is counting on me to follow the rules.
> *Client:* How can you put your boss ahead of me, your old friend and neighbor?
> *Bureaucrat:* (no answer)

The client appeals catalogued by Danet constitute challenges to the institution. New situations, new clients, new employees—all constitute a challenge. Unless the institution's structure is preserved by people at the appropriate stage, the institution will regress to less developed forms.

The Dynamic Consequences of Public Commonness

Development depends not just on cognitive stage levels but also on the relative visibility and feasibility of alternative cultural possibilities. Schelling's (1980:Chapter 3) "meeting problem" provides a physical metaphor for the cultural problem of establishing a publicly common way of relating. As Schelling presents it, the problem is that two people are to meet in a city, but they have made no prior arrangements when and where to meet and have no way to communicate with one another. What should they do to meet? Schelling's answer is that certain (largely accidental) features of times and places make them stand out as points of coordination. Noon, for example, is the time that most stands out during the day; the tallest building in town (or possibly city hall) is the most conspicuous place. This time and place therefore become the basis of coordination, not because they are "right" in any normative sense, but only because they stand out in some way. Noon may be inconvenient as a time to meet and the tallest building may be difficult to reach, but they are nonetheless the points required in order to guarantee mutuality of action.

Analogously, when two social actors interact, they both need a way of relating that is publicly common—common so that both can use it, publicly common so that interaction can take place without an elaborate preliminary search for common ground. How is one to know how to relate to others in a way accepted by all? The basis of a relationship can of course be established by negotiation without prior assumptions, but this is uncommon. There are usually several forces (the analogues of Schelling's "stand-out characteristics") that determine which way of relating is actually chosen. The first of these forces (cognitive stage) was discussed earlier: ways of relating that are too cognitively advanced cannot become publicly common if no one can grasp them. In addition, there are at least three other sets of forces at work affecting the choice: inertia, hegemony, and the presence of subcultures.

Public Commonness: Inertia

Inertia is undoubtedly the most powerful force affecting cultural choice. Existing cultures are supported by an enormous "sunk cost," both mental and physical. Consider the obstacles to be overcome by an instructor wishing to change the culture even of a college class. Psychologically, the students have put much effort into learning the existing college culture: that effort represents the mental cost invested in the culture. The students are each well-trained in existing modes of college instruction, successful in such modes of instruction, and unsure of the nature and consequences of alternative modes. Linguistically, the cultural terminology of "instructor" and "student" contemplates a particular mode of classroom experience. Physically, the classrooms are laid out with student desks all bolted to the floor to point in one direction. The blackboard is placed in front above a raised platform. The room's designers intended this arrangement to facilitate certain forms of interaction; their efforts represent the physical cost invested in the culture. One need not advocate stasis in order to recognize our cultural investment in it (Habermas, 1982:222-223).

Inertia has an even more basic force arising simply from the prior existence of the culture. The historical political culture (that is, the political culture up until yesterday) is the most obvious point of orientation for social actors. As Lukács (1914:321) puts it:

> Everything, once it appears in the world, takes on an existence entirely independent of its creator and purpose, its harmfulness or usefulness, its goodness or badness. . . . We are speaking here of the category of "being there" [*Bestehen*], naked existence as a force, a value, a decisively important category in the whole order of life (quoted in Arato and Breines, 1979:15).

New ways of relating, by contrast, have to be invented.

Concrete (experiential) history is therefore important in determining an individual's belief about the political culture. History gives rise to "anticipated reactions," affecting individuals in that their behavior is predicated on their belief about the political culture they share. They choose their actions in anticipation of their co-actors' reactions. The political culture as it has actually been experienced by social actors thus perpetuates the political culture. Inertia guarantees that the existing culture will always be the incumbent, so to speak, in any issue of cultural change.[9]

Public Commonness: Hegemony

Political regimes can rely on inertia to maintain themselves, but most prefer to give nature a hand, as it were, by exercising more direct influence over what ways of relating can become publicly common. The resulting forces I call "hegemonic."[10] A direct form of hegemonic force is exercised through rewards and punishments applied to the use of different ways of relating. The same power that allows privileged groups or classes to extract benefits for themselves can be used to maintain the culture against less favorable ways of relating: by rewarding cultural conformity and repressing dissent. This power of reward and sanction raises the ante needed to develop and promulgate new ways of relating.[11]

Rewards and punishments are costly, however. Rewards require direct outlays, and punishments require maintenance of a costly supervisory force. A more efficient form of hegemonic force is the differential exposure of various potential ways of relating and the differential invention and exploration of new cultural possibilities.[12] The choice of a way of relating is always made in view of the alternatives available and their acceptability to the partners. Public discussion of a cultural alternative is essential for the alternative to be commonly understood and thus capable of replacing the existing culture. If cultural alternatives are too ill-regarded to be mutually acceptable, too little-known to be mutually available, or simply not invented at all, then direct reward and repression are unnecessary.

Such forces have been studied by a variety of theorists under a variety of names. Socialization research has revealed biases built into U.S. school curricula and textbooks (Parenti, 1978:156-173, and 1983:41-44). Such biases are undoubtedly found elsewhere.[13] Overly (1970) discusses the role of the "hidden curriculum" (the way of relating actually practiced in the schools) as a source of learning more powerful than verbal education. (See also Parenti, 1983:41.) Bachrach and Baratz (1962) discuss "nondecision-making"—forces that act to prevent certain issues from becoming public issues. (For more recent discussions, see Wolfinger, 1971; Crenson, 1971; Stone, 1980, 1982.) Certain forms of nondecisions are kin to the Marxian concepts of "ideological" (class-based) thought and, as Wolfinger (1971) notes, "false consciousness." In the Marxian formulation, the ruling class's domination of the means of economic production results in their ability to dominate the means of intellectual production as well. (See Parenti, 1978:Part 2, for a description of this process.) The normative theories produced by intellectuals accordingly tend to justify the existing class structure; such class-limited philosophies are termed "ideology" in Marxian thought. Deprived of competing intellectual traditions, the proletariat or other dominated class comes to accept both the ruling class's ideology and its ideological interpretations of events. (See Lewy, 1982.)

Note that this discussion does not take any position in the long-standing debate between "pluralists" and "neo-elitists" over the importance of hegemonic forces for understanding U.S. society. The point is, rather, that such forces can exist, that they might have great weight, and, most important for this work, that they operate from mechanisms deriving from the require-ments of public commonness.[14]

Public Commonness: Subcultures

That a culture has a publicly common way of relating does not mean its members relate only in that way. Subsets of the culture can be subcultures: groups whose members choose a different way of relating. For example, people usually relate to other members of their immediate families not as fellow citizens but as intimates.

There is a continuum of subcultures between, on the one hand, those whose way of relating supplements and refines but does not set aside the tenets of the larger culture and, on the other hand, those whose way of relating supplants and denies the larger culture's claims. Examples of the former would include the Lions Clubs or a local church group: the larger culture looks benignly on the special ways these groups' members interrelate. Examples of the latter would include homosexual couples, whose way of relating to one another is illegal in many states.[15]

Subcultures are an important source of cultural innovation: they provide laboratories within which people can experiment with new ways of relating and new institutions. Because such experiments are confined to a restricted group, cultures find them relatively easy to tolerate as long as the participants remain duly respectful of the larger culture in their external relations.

The medieval city is a good example of how subcultures foster innovation. The city walls demarcated the subculture boundary (and enforced the tolerance of the city's feudal neighbors). Inside the city, new forms of social organization (e.g., craft guilds) were able to develop in a way they could not have in the wider, feudal culture. Ultimately, of course, the city subculture became strong enough simply to transform and even suppress the prior, feudal way of relating.

Subcultures are the cultural analogues of cognitive-developmental decalages: both contemplate domains differentially receptive to new cognitive structures. Some areas of the culture are easily adapted to new structure, while other areas may be quite resistant to any change, just as cognitive domains are.

Chapter 3 cited research indicating that moral reasoning decalage is quite restricted: people usually vary by no more than a single stage among different moral judgment problems or different aspects of the same problem. In addition, decalages are not very stable; they are, rather, a sign of an ongoing transition. Cultural decalages (subcultures), on the other hand, seem likely to be both more various and more stable. Relevant to this variance and stability are four sources of cultural decalage. First, social development has at least the same sources of decalage as cognitive development. If cognitive development to Stage X occurs first around one issue and only later around others, one would expect political development to show a similar decalage.[16] Second, the propagation of political development faces additional problems of space and cultural connection. Hot tubs show up in Scranton ten years after they do in California. Although our culture is relatively unitary, it consists of many more specialized subcultures linked only loosely by internal migration, by common tradition, by mass communication, by economic forces. As pluralists have long said, different political issues involve different constituencies. Third, the different constituencies are penetrated and integrated by different means. The practicalities of establishing a publicly common way of relating are different for a local union than for the recipients of Social Security benefits, and prison inmates must organize in different ways than garden clubs. Fourth, as Althusser (1970:esp.Chapter 4) points out at length, different social products have different logics and hence their own developmental rhythms. The production of social theory differs from the production of consumer goods, and both differ from the production of educated individuals. The differences will induce yet greater decalages. These variations show that political development should even more than cognitive development be subject to horizontal decalages.

Conclusion: Global Characteristics
of Developmental Dynamics

This chapter has presented a variety of dynamic forces, all arising from the requirements of cognitive structure and public commonness. These forces are inevitable—part of the general conditions of human culture.[17] Neolithic culture and twenty-fifth century culture appear equally subject to these forces. Because these forces govern the dynamics of social change and development, we can now address the five issues raised at the beginning of the chapter.

Unilinearity

Political development is unilinear in structure but multilinear in specific content. Social crises can have more than one developmental solution. Developmental trajectories can branch or converge.

Inevitability and the Role of Human Agency

The theory presented here yields no historical inevitability to development. It does argue that development is driven by, as Habermas (1979c:97) puts it, "a gentle but obstinate, a never silent although seldom redeemed claim to reason, a claim that must be recognized de facto whenever and wherever there is to be consensual action." This steady force for development is (in Piagetian terms) the force of cognitive equilibration or (in cultural terms) the drive to resolve ambiguities and contradictions in the cultural way of relating.

However, such a force is only one of several acting on the political culture. Just as the cognitive development of individuals is not inevitable but rather dependent upon the recognition of conflicts and the mental time and energy to resolve them, so is the political development of cultures dependent upon accidents of nature and society.

The overall political development of the past ten thousand years indicates that the steady force of cognitive equilibration has an effect. This force is not a physical or impersonal "march of history," however. Instead, it is a force constituted and reconstituted anew by people who in a performative attitude affirm the existence of a social (moral) truth rather than in a propositional attitude recognizing the existence of an objective truth. (See Habermas, 1979a, 1979d.) It is this force that requires that development theorists take normative beliefs seriously. Theorists must study beliefs for their normative impact and thus their value, not just their objective structure.

Monotonicity, Devolution, and Cycles

Both Binder et al. (1971:esp.297-307) and (Grew 1978:esp.10-34) see development as proceeding in a discontinuous fashion; that is, in periods of crisis followed by periods of consolidation. The definition of a crisis may be subject to discussion, and a certain amount of retrogression may occur, but these works view crises as basically irreversible. Grew (1978:11): Changes "must now appear to have been *in some sense irreversible.*" Pye, in his introduction to Grew (1978:vii-viii): "Even [the] complaint [that the same crisis can repeatedly return] . . . is qualified by the acknowledgement that there is a 'ratchet effect,' that is, societies cannot go back and pretend that changes have not taken place."

Despite these contentions, the present theory indicates that political cultures can regress. If the average adult moral reasoning stage declines, the political culture of the society may well decline, having fewer higher-stage people to support its previous high levels and having more lower-stage people to fail to understand it. Even in the absence of any overall decline, the accidents of history may give hegemonic power to a regime dedicated to the imposition of a regressive way of relating. (Obvious examples include external invasions and the rise of a leader like Hitler.) However, since there is a steady force for development and none for regression, the overall trend should be upward.

This work's analysis yields no dynamics creating long-term cycles of development and regression. Certainly development and regression can succeed one another, giving the appearance of a cyclical historical trajectory, but there seems to be no basis for our expecting any inevitable cyclical motion.

Asynchrony

This analysis provides a means of discussing political develop-
ent without necessary reference to nation-states or any other
fixed entity. (As Grew, 1978:5, states the problem: "In most of
the literature on modernization the favorite unit of analysis—
the national state—is not that in which the subject of analysis,
social change, occurs.") We can conceive of any society as a set of
hierarchically organized, overlapping, and differentially
articulated cultures. (See Althusser, 1970:esp. Chapter 4.) The
social scientist's task is then the analysis of the ways of relating
publicly common within each (sub)culture and the determination of the dynamics and cross-linkages of those
(sub)cultures.

Does development proceed independently in different areas
of our culture? Certainly total independence is impossible as
long as there are free communicative links within the culture as
a whole. At the very least, individual cognitive development,
stimulated by the example from more developed subcultures,
should eventually result in the transformation of the broader
culture.

It is apparent, however, that the decalages of development
between groups can be large. Hegemonic control of communication, in addition to all the other sources of within-culture
variation, may result in much wider stage variations in political
development than are seen in individual cognitive development.
Thus development need not occur equally and simultaneously
throughout a society. The existence of subcultures, and the
imperfect linkage of cultural areas with one another—both
allow developmental decalages to occur.

Continuity, Crises, and Stage Skipping

Do societies develop smoothly, or in leaps stimulated by crises?
From the present perspective, the question appears to have no
determinate answer, because a developmental history will
depend on which culture/subculture is chosen from the "set of
hierarchically organized, overlapping, and differentially
articulated cultures" mentioned above. Certainly it is possible to
have discontinuous development, as Binder et al. (1971) and

Grew (1978) show in numerous examples. A widely felt cultural challenge that demands immediate response (e.g., a war) can create a developmental discontinuity as the entire culture is transformed at once. On the other hand, if the culture being studied is diverse enough and the crisis it faces requires no immediate resolution, then development may appear continuous, as the (possibly discontinuous) alterations of the constituent subcultures aggregate into the appearance of smooth flow. (Duby, 1977:esp. p.218, discusses social change along these lines. Grew, 1978:10-15, discusses possible criteria for calling a period or event a "crisis.")

In cognitive development the individual never skips a stage in the process of development—each stage builds on the one previous to it. Is the same true of political development? Clearly stage skipping is not possible when a culture first develops to a specific stage. Just as each cognitive stage must build on the one before, each new level of culture must grow out of the one immediately previous. No matter what the cognitive levels of the individuals are in the society, they would appear to need time to work out the practical social problems of one level of development before proceeding to the next.

One can imagine, however, that stage skipping would be possible in certain other circumstances. If a culture were conquered by a two-stage-lower culture and were shortly thereafter freed, the first culture would be able to spring back to its original stage. The longer the second culture's domination lasted, however, the less likely such a return would be: children would increasingly orient to the new culture and would be unsure how to relate in the old culture; and the changes accumulating with the new regime would make the exact restoration of the old regime ever less appropriate.

The Complexity of Developmental Dynamics

The above discussion shows that development is an extremely complex process. This does not mean simply that many forces (e.g., literacy, communication, military ambitions, etc.) affect development, for that has long been known. It means, rather, that development occurs through the interaction of profoundly dissimilar forces: forces inducing cognitive development and social invention, forces of social inertia, forces of hegemonic control, and forces of subgroup/subculture interaction. Within cognitive development itself, each stage differs from all other stages in its cognitive ambiguities, and so a theory of political development must embrace at least five structurally dissimilar transitional forms of the moral reasoning alone. The six different structural forms of societies may each take social form in an infinite number of distinct institutional arrangements, each yielding unique transitions.

The variety of cognitive transitions will be further diffracted by the wholly separate variety of inertial and hegemonic forces by which the existing culture is maintained. Would Gandhi have succeeded if India had been Nazi Germany's colony and not England's? Certainly Martin Luther King's tactics had greater success against Bull Connor's police power than against the Chicago financial elite's economic power. There are a variety of instruments of hegemonic control and circumstances making them possible, and the specifics of political development will be accordingly complex.

This interaction explains why simple theories of political development have been doomed to failure. Development has complex dynamics: societies can advance or decline or simply change; they can advance in jerks or smoothly; in exceptional circumstances they can skip stages; they can advance on some fronts and not on others. Even though development theorists have pointed to similar sequences of developmental stages, none have explained developmental dynamics properly. Hobhouse, for example, was reduced to speculating about the survival of the morally fittest society—a reflection of his time's Social Darwinism. Theories of simple unilinear progression cannot encompass development's complexity.

The theoretical outline presented here does not deny that complexity. Instead, it offers analysts a relatively simple framework for explaining how their unique events arise. Even though each of the dynamic forces are complex in themselves, they are much simpler than their interaction, and clearly identifying their effects will enable researchers to find unifying themes. To take just one example, I referred above to the variety of social forms existing at Stage 3 and noted that there would be a corresponding variety of transitions to Stage 4. It is quite possible that these transitions will resemble one another —that their common origins in the structural ambiguity of Stage 3 will give rise to common transitions. If so, such common transitions may react to hegemonic forms in equally characteristic ways.

These possibilities are mere speculations here, of course, but they indicate in what direction researchers will most likely find results. We know from bitter empirical experience and from the present theoretical outline that development occurs in many ways; we need to seek simplification through the natural terms of the processes creating such variety.

Notes

1. Not surprisingly, but pleasing nevertheless, these dynamics arise from the solutions to what was earlier termed the two major theoretical challenges facing political development conceptions: the challenges of normative grounding and of making the micro-macro connection.

2. During the mid-1970s the American Chemical Society's *Chemical and Engineering News*—analogous to political scientists' *PS*—carried a year-long exchange of letters between dogmatic creationists and dogmatic "scientists."

3. Döbert (1975), in his attempt to apply a genetic-epistemological model to religious beliefs, discusses what "knowledge" (i.e., "an 'independent' environment" to which belief systems must adapt) means in the context of religion. He argues that "God" is not the appropriate target of such knowledge since God "is always anew constituted by the developing patterns of religious consciousness." Döbert (1975:10-12) suggests that the necessary target of knowledge can be found in Luckmann's (1963) view of religion as one element of meaning in "a process of constituting and maintaining society."

4. This thesis is discussed in Robinson (1976), cited in Hennessy (1985:244-246).

5. See, for example, the research reported in Pye (1963).

6. Such difficulties may, however, be more potential than actual in concrete circumstances. For example, a civil war between equally matched adherents of two Stage 4 legal systems could be "resolved" by a turn to the authority of a widespread religious fundamentalism. The latter might ignore the few religious groups not sharing its tenets, but this structural defect can be concealed by oppression in a way that the civil war was only attempting to do.

7. I am indebted to Fred Frey for first calling my attention to the concept of social inversions.

8. Habermas (1979c:99) calls this "the background consensus of habitual daily routine."

9. This is why history, even as an academic field, is so politically sensitive. As a substitute in political socialization for concrete (experiential) history, academic history creates the future political

culture in its reconstruction of the past.

10. I am indebted to Clarence Stone (1980, 1982, and personal communication) for clarifying my thinking about the various aspects of hegemonic power.

11. This form of power generally corresponds to Stone's (1982:286) "second level of power." His "first level of power" involves activities taken within an established cultural context (that is, the playing out of a given way of relating) and so does not concern us in the present discussion of developmental choices among alternative ways of relating.

12. This form of power generally corresponds to Stone's (1982:286) "third level of power."

13. See, for example, Bronfenbrenner's (1962) study of Soviet education.

14. The debate over the presence of hegemonic forces only partly concerns empirical evidence. As Ono (1965:52) notes (cited in Wolfinger, 1971:1078), empirical evidence cannot discriminate between the neo-elitist and pluralist models. Wolfinger admits the possible existence of hegemonic forces, and argues that neo-elitist models can only be researched from a prior normative commitment. He concludes from this that such research should not be undertaken, since normative questions are outside the social-scientific purview. Without pursuing the question further, I would argue that normative issues can be studied, if not in the ways Wolfinger seems to accept, and that it seems odd for a social scientist like Wolfinger to recognize a potentially important social force and then simply refuse to study it. As Chapter 1 proposes, we must make normative grounding a criterion of our research and see where it leads us.

15. For the sake of the example we here assume that the United States as a whole has a single culture, which of course it does not, and that laws define the culture, which of course they do not.

16. The decalages of moral development seem likely to be the traces of previous social crises. If so, cognitive development will recapitulate social development in the ordering of cognitive acquisitions.

17. They would be known to the actors in Rawls's (1971) Original Position, for example.

SIX

Theoretical Implications

Linkages with Political Development's Intellectual Heritage

This work arose from my conviction that earlier formulations have gone astray in ways too subtle to revise directly. I therefore began it not with previous definitions of political development, about which there is much disagreement,[1] but rather with previous challenges, which offer more unanimity. Without immediately presuming to judge earlier work as correct or incorrect, I sought to start afresh by a return to the fundamental theoretical challenges facing political development conceptions. Because these challenges presuppose no special theoretical perspective and rely on no empirical claim, I felt an honest solution to them should provide firm theoretical ground from which to assess prior efforts. We are now in a position to carry out that assessment by looking at how the present theoretical framework is related to previous and current usages of the political development concept.

Two usages we can dismiss out of hand. The first is the identification of political development with Westernization, economic growth, industrialization, modernization, and the like. As Pye (1966a:36-37) puts it, the confusion between political development and Westernization "runs into the difficulty of differentiating between what is 'Western' and what is ['developed.']"[2] Nevertheless, such confusion continues to appear, e.g., in Khalilzad (1984-5) and Bianchi (1984).

A second, clearly incorrect usage employs the term "political development" in the sense of political developments—mere occurrences or change,[3] even though the strong normative connotations of "development" demand its distinction from "change." For example, Plascov (1982) never defines political development, but only implies that it is whatever happens politically during social modernization. Bensel (1984), a historian, fails to define the "political development" of his book's title, appearing to regard it as "historical events and trends." Auster and Silver (1979) say merely that political structures transform themselves, but the authors do not distinguish development from mere change. The term "development" does not appear in any of these works' indexes. Ironically, this usage resists Huntington's (1971) call for "a change to [the study of] change" while simultaneously adding to the confusion surrounding the term development that Huntington cites as the primary reason to abandon it.

Having dismissed the obviously incorrect usages of the concept, we are still left with a variety of conceptions having substantial merit. How are these related to the present theoretical framework? We will examine first the related Hegelian and Marxian approaches, second the related progress theory and cultural relativist approaches, and finally, the Social Science Research Council's Committee on Comparative Politics' formulation.[4] The discussions are inevitably cursory, but I think they cover the central connections.

To Hegel, history reflects human beings' progressively greater "consciousness of freedom," or "spirit," which is seen in many aspects of intellectual activity (e.g., religion; philosophy) and which is objectivated in corresponding social and political institutions. Hegel's idealist conception of the origins of institutions is closely related to the present work's conception of institutions as organized through moral reasoning structures. In the present framework, Hegel's almost metaphorical (or, as Marx termed it, mystified) concepts of "spirit" and "consciousness of freedom" take more concrete meanings as cognitive structures which coordinate, more or less successfully, different moral perspectives. This framework identifies the Hegelian dialectic as the cognitive growth process arising from a single stage's ambiguities.

The present conception connects at several points with Marx's theory of development. First, its approach to development is dialectical, as Hegel's was, but is also grounded in material relations, as Marx's was. The cognitive-structural ambiguities referred to in the previous paragraph appear in their cultural manifestations as concrete contradictions between actors in different social positions. Marx criticized the idealist foundations of the Hegelian dialectic, which was drawn upward by an ideal (that is, preserving what was true in both a thesis and its negation) rather than constructed layer by layer out of real, conflicting positions. The Piagetian epistemology that underlies cognitive development also sees knowledge as constructed and, even closer to Marx's position, as constructed out of manipulations of the material environment. Such manipulations occur only at early stages of the child's development, however. They are later replaced by "operational" thought, which organizes symbolic representations of more material action. This symbolic activity is the centerpiece of Habermas's (1979:esp.pp.97-98) reconstruction of Marxian thought through the concept of communicative action. That reconstruction, and the present framework, thus preserve Marx's materialist, constructivist epistemology while still recognizing, as Hegel does, a role for purely intellectual activity. In the Piagetian epistemology, intellectual activity is a continuation of material activity by other, more interior means.

Second, the present analytic framework reveals specific mechanisms whereby a ruling class is able to maintain its dominance: partly by controlling public commonness, and partly by inhibiting reasoning beyond the existing cognitive structure. Thus, like Marx's, the present theory sees an interplay between ideas and real social forces. To draw the parallel more closely, ideas constitute the Marxian "relations of production," which underlie all aspects of society, not simply its economic aspect. The social forces aiding or inhibiting the establishment of new ways of relating are the forces of production. There is some debate among Marxian scholars over the nature of such forces (e.g., do they arise solely from technological change?); the present framework sees them as, broadly, whatever forces advance or restrict the public commonness (or potential public commonness) of any way of relating. Like Marx, the present framework sees development arising from the interaction of the relations of production and the forces of production, but it also sees a force for development arising from the internal, moral ambiguities of the relations of production.

Third, the present theory rejects the "vulgar Marxist" image of an economic base and a political-social-ideological super-structure. The differentiation of structure and content clarifies the interconnection of different facets of the social whole: a given structure can permeate all the above-mentioned aspects of a culture, with their mutual interactions dependent on specifics of institutional inventiveness and adaptability (horizontal decalage, in cognitive terms) and cultural hegemony (which has no cognitive counterpart). Marx may have argued that the means of production are the most useful for hegemonic control, being most directly important to physical survival, but that proposition is unnecessary to Marx's general theory.[5]

Fourth, the present approach reconciles Marx's claims to scientific status with political development's normative connotations. That reconciliation arises from the dual empirical and normative claims of Kohlberg's work.

We now turn briefly to the progress theorists, who claim a steady progress in human affairs, and to the cultural relativists, who support their philosophical claim that cultures can only be judged by the cultures' own standards with the empirical observation that different cultures have different standards and different historical patterns. The present theory reconciles somewhat restructured versions of these positions. It recasts the cultural relativists' philosophical claim as the Kantian criterion of universalizability: the normative foundation of any conception of development must respect the moral claims of all social actors. In particular, it must respect cultural integrity to the extent that any culture has a right to have it respected.[6] This formulation of the cultural relativists' claim relieves them from holding the unprovable metaethical position that non-relativistic judgments cannot be made. The present conception of development does show that different cultures can develop along different developmental paths—of different content, that is, but not of different structure.

Progress theories are likewise somewhat restructured. Progress is not inevitable, due to problems of establishing public commonness, but there is a developmental force, arising from individual cognitive development and preference for higher stages.[7] The patterns of legal-ethical development observed by Hobhouse (1906) are therefore probably not fortuitous but a reflection of a more general developmental process. Nevertheless, the route of progress depends upon the specific culture's specific contradictions.

We turn finally to a more recent attempt to conceptualize political development: the influential work of the Committee on Comparative Politics of the Social Science Research Council (SSRC-CCP). The volume and variety of work in that tradition makes it difficult to characterize.[8] It is fair to say, however, that the entire approach uses Parsonian pattern variables to characterize and grade different political systems. In Pye's famous "development syndrome" list (1966a:45-48), the pattern variables of development are "equality," "differentiation," and "capacity." Rightly refusing to become mired in problems of operationalization or of tradeoffs among the variables, Pye argues that these three broadly understood variables characterize political development. Later research in the SSRC-CCP tradition adds various operationalizations and combinations of these variables and produces many specific findings, but it seems fair to say that Pye's basic perspective continues to inform the tradition.

The present conception of development closely resembles Pye's, if we interpret equality, differentiation, and capacity as criteria of moral reasoning rather than as pattern variables. First, equality is readily interpreted as the ethical criterion of universalizability. This becomes plain in Pye's (1966a:45-46) discussion of the various facets of equality. The first facet—popular participation—follows from universalizability's demand that the political system be fair from the perspective of the people as well as government officials. The second facet—a universalistic, impersonal legal system—follows from universalizability's elimination of invidious distinctions, as does the third facet—achievement rather than ascriptive standards. Pye's various facets of equality all seem to derive from the broader criterion of universalizability. Use of that criterion avoids the more specific, content-laden (and thus potentially ethnocentric) formulations that Pye employs.

The demand for equality arises from our basic ethical belief that morally similar cases be treated similarly. Pye's second pattern variable, differentiation, can be interpreted as the ethical demand that morally different cases be treated differently. Pye calls attention to two facets of the term. The first facet—differentiation as division of labor or of legal function—seems unrelated to development. Division of labor or legal function may be a good idea in many circumstances, but it has no inherent normative significance. The second facet—

differentiation as a finer mesh in a coherent net of political arrangements[9]—seems much closer to development. The complexity of moral considerations in society requires a differentiation of moral cases within a coherent, just way of relating. Such a differentiation may involve actual specialization of political functions, as in a complex bureaucracy, or it might simply mean that the culture's way of relating must contain relevant complexity. Differentiation thus can be a criterion of development, not for its own sake, but only to the extent that it reflects the complexity of actual ethical considerations. To seek differentiation without such guidance is, again, to run the risk of ethnocentrism.

Pye's third pattern variable is capacity. He uses the term in two senses, one denoting "the sheer magnitude, scope, and scale of political and governmental performance" (1966a:46), the second denoting the secular rationality, effectiveness, and efficiency of governmental performance, regardless of its extent. The present conception views these two senses as quite distinct. First, the extent or scope of politics or government has no inherent virtue, so theorists cannot regard it as a criterion of development but only as a contingent byproduct.[10] Nevertheless, this sense of capacity has theoretical meaning in the present conception, where capacity is seen as another term for public commonness. From Pye's viewpoint, capacity breaks down in states like, say, Niger or Chad, where nomadic, "parochial" tribes have no sense of citizenship and wander freely across international borders. In the present conception, such tribes merely illustrate that the Western way of relating (in terms of states, boundaries, laws, and so on) is not publicly common. What is publicly common is the use of force, or bribery, or whatever means the central government finds it must employ. Thus, *taken as a whole,* Niger, Chad, and other "low-capacity" states are indeed not developed.[11] In other words, Pye is concerned about capacity-as-scope for the same reasons as the present conception is concerned about culture-as-publicly-common.

Pye's second sense of capacity is of government's rational connection between means and ends, resulting in greater political effectiveness and efficiency. The connection between this and moral reasoning development can be seen most easily if we ask: What general characteristics of interpersonal relationships create effectiveness and efficiency? Those characteristics turn out to be precisely those of the different cognitive stages: an organization can be more effective and efficient when people can coordinate each other's perspectives (Stage 3), when such mutual relationships are coordinated with one another (Stage 4), and when such coordinated structures are "based on [Stage 5] rational calculation of overall utility" (Kohlberg, 1981c:412).

In sum, the present theoretical framework has close links with several major, earlier traditions of development, including traditions usually seen as opposed to one another (Hegel's and Marx's) and even a tradition apparently unalterably opposed to any concept of development (cultural relativism). Despite the very disparate nature of these traditions, the linkages drawn are not strained but are, rather, quite natural. In some cases they appear to clarify the earlier tradition; in no case do they appear to distort it.

Some Residual Notes

The perspective presented in this work has certain implications, or consequences, or advantages, which do not pertain directly to (narrowly construed) political development, but which deserve mention because of their theoretical, ethical, or practical importance.

Social Science and the Concept of Human Nature

Social-scientific theories get into trouble when they depend on a specific view of human nature. Such views reflect the cultural origins of both the theorists and their subjects, so that: subjects "naturally" express culturally conditioned behavior; this behavior is understood by researchers in the culture's context (as subjects intend it to be); and then it is cited as empirical proof of theories that people are innately like the culture requires them to be. There thus arises a circularity of theory and proof: cultural behavior supports theories of innate character, and these theories justify the culture. This circularity inhibits any critical/emancipatory theory of human nature as it is and might be: cultural deviants become "error variance" or "outliers" instead of small but important indicators of cultural possibility.

Any assumption that human beings are inherently a certain way denies that people can see, evaluate, and change the way they relate to one another. That is to say, such perspectives deny the possibility of raising (or answering, if raised) the open question: "Is it right?" The present theoretical framework admits that humans are molded by the cultural ways of relating, but it also shows that such ways of relating are subject to the open question. People who daily experience one way of relating will obviously be hard put to question it or, if they do, to answer the questions raised, but the possibility remains. Theories assuming one form of human nature will only work until the next cultural transformation.[12]

The consequence of this perspective is that social science must itself be a developing organism.[13] If culture changes, then rules of behavior will also change, and the "laws" of social science will have to change with them. Even before such changes occur, however, it would be well for social science to recognize in its basic theory the possibility of such change. The framework presented in this work recognizes that possibility.

Developing U.S. Culture

I argued earlier that normative theory cannot be divorced from empirical description. It should be no surprise, then, that the perspective given in this work has normative as well as empirical implications. In this section, I will sketch those implications and apply them to a critique of U.S. society. I make no claim to the novelty of the critique; I advance it first because the reader may wish to see the implication of this work's perspective, and second because the critique might be more comprehensible for some when viewed from this perspective.

The phrase "ways of relating" implies more than such alternative phrases as, say, "plans of action" or "systems of strategic behavior." The phrase implies action in a mutual relationship, and thereby acknowledges that culture is created by all of us relating in the cultural way. Whether such relating is born of fear, or mere passivity, or enthusiastic support, the same culture is created.

When we collectively create the cultural conditions of a society, we bear the responsibility for how it affects each of us.

Undoubtedly there are impersonal constraints on us: of existing knowledge, of the physical world. Within such constraints, however, it is we who create cultures. Individually we may feel powerless to change a culture, but collectively we are responsible for our creation.

How are we to relate to one another? Currently, we have created a system in which certain human characteristics (e.g., brains) usually are rewarded and certain others (e.g., brawn) usually are not, or not as much. Even if we assume a procedurally fair system, where education or other training is open to all and discrimination does not exist except on the basis of job capacity, extreme differences of wealth and poverty can arise from accidents of intelligence, parental guidance, and life history. Moreover, such social extremes can arise regardless of personal virtue. Arguments like "if she had worked harder (or smarter), she'd have been better off" are beside the point, because in our current political-social-economic system, even if we were all workaholic geniuses our society would still have its rich and poor according to the impersonal market forces we collectively create and submit to. The contention that failure is the sign of bad judgment (or other personal flaw) is a tautology. How do we know who has bad judgment?—by who fails. Why do people fail?—because they have bad judgment. Such a tautology cannot be a principle of moral evaluation.

What we have done as a culture is turn over our moral decisions about how we are to relate to one another to an impersonal, arbitrary mechanism called "market efficiency," and we pretend to ourselves that we have no obligations to one another beyond the maintenance of that culture. But in any culture, including ours, members should be able to face one another and be able to say: "You and I created our culture this way; we are doing it together; and we can look at each other as sisters and brothers." Our culture's dirty little secret is that we cannot say this; its stability rests on our having convinced ourselves and our society's failures that they deserved to fail.

Development and Foreign Policy

As all political development theorists know, the "Decade of Development" did not produce much development. Economies did not grow, or else populations grew faster; democracies fell, or never arrived at all. From the perspective of this work, this lack of development is understandable; quite simply, development is difficult. Cognitive development is difficult enough, even in a society that encourages it, and public commonness is even more difficult—a new way of relating must be widely learned, in the absence of examples, and must become a common focus, despite all hegemonic forces arrayed against it. That cultures change at all seems amazing.

This perspective has implications for our development policy and, more generally, our foreign policy. First, it implies that we should be more reasonable in our expectations of other societies. Stage X cultures will not become Stage X+3, or even X+1, overnight. We are certainly free to criticize or even to act to prevent practices that are wrong according to universalizable principles of justice, but it is pointless to blame or condemn other societies for them.

Second, a development policy is best targeted at developing moral reasoning, not at eliciting pro-American attitudes, trade concessions, or military bases. Our ability to maintain an effective development policy may depend on these attitudes, concessions, and bases, but the danger is always that the tail winds up wagging the dog.

Third, even if cultures are at different levels of development, the theory does not imply that the less-developed culture must become like the more developed. Development policy is best targeted at fostering indigenous developmental resolutions to a culture's indigenous problems, not at imposing Western institutions. Cognitive development only occurs when the reasoner finds and resolves ambiguities and contradictions within her own cognitive structure. Social development therefore depends on a nation's widespread recognition of its own culture's ambiguities and contradictions. Western institutions may in some cases provide appropriate solutions to such problems, but we must recognize that the primary criterion of a development policy must be cultural appropriateness. Any other criterion simply reflects our exercise of hegemonic control.

As a consequence, fourth, our policy should aid indigenous and progressive movements, not alien, regressive, or repressive movements. We must take ideologies more seriously as reflecting the emergence into consciousness of certain cultural contradictions. This consciousness cannot be suppressed without moral (possibly physical) violence; it would appear that the best we can do is stay out of the gears while they turn. Our support of reactionary, repressive regimes (e.g., the Somoza dynasty in Nicaragua) against strong, popular movements pointing out real problems has been short-sighted. We gain a decade or so of stable repression in the country, enabling U.S. businesses briefly to make money, but we lose our international reputation and, ultimately, our self-respect as an agent of development. The issue is not whether we should ally ourselves with backward governments: clearly there are many such whose alliance is desirable. The true issue is rather our unwillingness to abandon these alliances when popular opposition to the government crystalizes. Like bad politicians, we find ourselves backing losers over and over again. The public justifications for our policies are given as proving America's "will," "determination," or "commitment to its allies," but the real effect seems only to be to make the United States look foolish.

Finally, this perspective shows that our moral concerns cannot stop "at the water's edge": our way of relating to people in other countries is, like relations within our society, constructed and mutual. We cannot evade sharing the collective responsibility for the way all people in the world relate to one another.

Notes

1. See, for example, the variety of definitions cited in Pye (1966); Jaguaribe (1973); Riggs (1981); and Park (1984).

2. Pye goes on to note that "additional criteria seem to be necessary if such a distinction is to be made." The only such criteria evident to me are the structural ones discussed in Chapters 3 and 4.

3. In some cases the term will appear only in a book or article's title: an intellectual orchid that provides decoration to its surroundings but no strength to its host. For example, the concept "development" vanishes after Burg's (1984) title, "Muslim Cadres and Soviet Political Development."

4. We will not specifically discuss the dependency theory approach. The discussion of Marxian approaches in general should indicate the links between the present conception and dependency theory. I apologize in advance to adherents of theoretical approaches not discussed here.

5. Similarly, Lukács (1971:1) argues that the validity of Marxism does not hang on the verification of even one of Marx's theses.

6. Clearly the right to have one's culture's integrity respected is

not absolute. The German culture had no right to exterminate its Jews, Gypsies, and so on. No culture has a right to human sacrifice. Judgments concerning cultural integrity cannot be made casually, running the clear risk of cultural imperialism, but we must recognize that they can be made.

7. Social-scientific theories of why development occurs or does not occur can be constructed, but they cannot reconceptualize development itself.

8. See, for example, the varying approaches taken by Binder et al. (1971); Grew (1978); Pye (1966a); Almond and Coleman (1960); and Almond and Powell (1966). Holt and Turner (1975) review the corpus of CCP work through Binder et al. (1971).

9. Pye (1966a:47): ". . . differentiation is not fragmentation and the isolation of the different parts of the political system but specialization based on an ultimate sense of integration."

10. This goes back to Chapter 1's argument that the line between the political and nonpolitical is difficult to draw. The line we now draw is, in my estimation, only a culturally conditioned optical illusion. At least currently, the only defensible position is to see all aspects of ways of relating as ethically significant and thus political.

11. It may be that these states have a quite developed political culture if one considers only those groups around the capital cities.

12. This explains an important aspect of John Rawls's (1971) theory of justice. Rawls makes a determined effort not to introduce any concept of "human nature" behind his Veil of Ignorance. There may be endless discussion of how moral discourse can proceed without such a concept, but this appears to have been his basic intent. Gramsci (1957:140) similarly asserts that Marx introduced no concept of human nature into his theory, regarding it instead as determined by the economic relations characteristic of the existing mode of production.

13. As Gramsci (1957) also argues. (See note 12.)

Bibliography

Abrams, Philip (1982) *Historical Sociology* (Ithaca, NY: Cornell University Press).

Almond, Gabriel, and James S. Coleman (eds) (1960) *The Politics of the Developing Areas* (Princeton, NJ: Princeton University Press).

Almond, Gabriel, and G. Bingham Powell (1966) *Comparative Politics: A Developmental Approach* (Boston: Little, Brown).

Almond, Gabriel, and Sidney Verba (1963) *The Civic Culture: Political Attitudes and Democracy in Five Nations* (Princeton, NJ: Princeton University Press).

Althusser, Louis (1970) "The Object of *Capital*" in Louis Althusser and Étienne Balibar, *Reading Capital* (trans. by Ben Brewster) (London: Verso Editions), pp.71-198.

Apter, David E. (1968) *Some Conceptual Approaches to the Study of Modernization* (Englewood Cliffs, NJ: Prentice-Hall).

Arato, Andrew, and Paul Breines (1979) *The Young Lukács and the Origins of Western Marxism* (New York: Seabury).

Armon, Cheryl (1984) "Ideals of the Good Life and Moral Judgment: Evaluative Reasoning in Children and Adults" *Moral Education Forum* 9(2):1-27.

Aronoff, Joel (1967) *Psychological Needs and Cultural Systems: A Case Study* (Princeton, NJ: Van Nostrand).

—— (1970) "Psychological Needs as a Determinant in the Formations of Economic Structures: A Confirmation" *Human Relations* 23(2, April):123-138.

Auster, Richard D., and Morris Silver (1979) *The State as a Firm: Economic Forces in Political Development* (Boston: Martinus Nijhoff).

Bachrach, Peter, and Morton Baratz (1962) "The Two Faces of Power" *American Political Science Review* 56:947-952.

Benedict, Ruth (1946) *The Chrysanthemum and the Sword*

113

(Cambridge, MA: Houghton Mifflin).

Bensel, Richard F. (1984) *Sectionalism and American Political Development 1880-1980* (Madison, WI: University of Wisconsin Press).

Berti, Anna Emilia, Anna Silvia Bombi, and Rossana De Beni (1986) "Acquiring Economic Notions: Profit" *International Journal of Behavioral Development* 9:15-29.

Berti, Anna Emilia, Anna Silvia Bombi, and Adriana Lis (1982) "The Child's Conceptions about Means of Production and Their Owners" *European Journal of Social Psychology* 12:221-239.

Bertilson, H., D. Springer, and K. Fierke (1982) "Underrepresentation of Female Referents as Pronouns, Examples and Pictures in Introductory College Textbooks" *Psychological Reports* 51:923-931.

Bianchi, Robert (1984) *Interest Groups and Political Development in Turkey* (Princeton, NJ: Princeton University Press).

Binder, Leonard, et al. (1971) *Crises and Sequences in Political Development* (Princeton, NJ: Princeton University Press).

Bloch, Marc (1961) *Feudal Society: The Growth of Ties of Dependence, and Social Classes and Political Organization* (trans. by L.A. Manyon and published in two volumes) (Chicago: University of Chicago Press).

Bronfenbrenner, Urie (1962) "Soviet Methods of Character Education: Some Implications for Research" *American Psychologist* 17:550-565.

Brown, Archie (1977) "Introduction" in Archie Brown and Jack Gray (eds), *Political Culture and Political Change in Communist States* (New York: Holmes and Meier).

Burg, Steven L. (1984) "Muslim Cadres and Soviet Political Development: Reflections from a Comparative Perspective" *World Politics* 37(1):24-47.

Chesler, Robert (1983) "Imagery of Community, Ideology of Authority: The Moral Reasoning of Chief Justice Burger" *Harvard Civil Rights—Civil Liberties Law Review* 18:457-482.

Chilcote, Ronald (1981) "Theories of Development and Underdevelopment" in Ronald Chilcote, *Theories of Comparative Politics: The Search for a Paradigm* (Boulder, CO: Westview), pp.271-346.

Chilton, Stephen (1977) *The Analysis of Power Structures in Three High Schools* (Unpublished Ph.D. dissertation, Cambridge, MA: Massachusetts Institute of Technology).

———— (1987) "Defining Political Culture" (mimeo).

Colby, Ann (1976) "The Relationship between Logical and Moral Development" (Unpublished manuscript, Cambridge, MA: Center for Moral Education, Harvard University).

Colby, Ann, and Lawrence Kohlberg (forthcoming) *The Measurement of Moral Judgment* (2 volumes) (New York: Oxford University

Press).

Colby, Ann, Lawrence Kohlberg, John Gibbs, and Marcus Lieberman (1983) *A Longitudinal Study of Moral Judgment. Monographs of the Society for Research in Child Development* 48(1, Serial No. 200).

Crenson, Matthew (1971) *The Un-Politics of Air Pollution: A Study of Non-Decisionmaking in the Cities* (Baltimore, MD: Johns Hopkins University Press).

Danet, Brenda (1971) "The Language of Persuasion in Bureaucracy: 'Modern' and 'Traditional' Appeals to the Israel Customs Authorities" *American Sociological Review* 36(October):847-859.

Davies, James Chowning (1977) "The Priority of Human Needs and the Stages of Political Development" in J. Roland Pennock and John W. Chapman (eds), *Human Nature in Politics* (New York: New York University Press), pp.157-196.

—————— (1986) "Roots of Political Behavior" in Margaret B. Hermann (ed), *Political Psychology* (San Francisco: Jossey-Bass), pp.39-61.

Deutsch, Karl W. (1961) "Social Mobilization and Political Development" *American Political Science Review* 55:493-514.

Deutsch, Karl W., Jorge I. Dominguez, and Hugh Heclo (1981) *Comparative Government: Politics of Industrialized and Developing Nations* (Boston, MA: Houghton Mifflin).

DeVries, Rheta, and Lawrence Kohlberg (1977) "Relations between Piaget and Psychometric Assessments of Intelligence" in L. Katz (ed), *Current Topics in Early Childhood Education Vol. I* (Norwood, NJ: Ablex).

Dobelstein, Andrew W. (1985) "The Bifurcation of Social Work and Social Welfare: The Political Development of Social Services" *Urban and Social Change Review* 18:9-12.

Döbert, Rainer (1975) "'Modern Religion' and the Relevance of Religious Movements: Pleadings for an Evolutionary Approach" (Paper presented at the Second International Symposium on Belief, Baden bei Wien BRD, January 8-11). This paper is published as "Religione moderna e movimenti religiosi: per un approccio evoluzionistico" in R. Caporale (ed) (1976), *Vecci e unovi Dei* (Torino, Italy: Editoirale Valentino).

—————— (1981) "The Role of Stage Models within a Theory of Social Evolution, Illustrated by the European Witch Craze" in U.J. Jensen and R. Harre (eds), *The Philosophy of Evolution* (Brighton, Sussex: Harvester Press), pp.71-119.

Dorsey, John T., Jr. (1963) "The Bureaucracy and Political Development in Viet Nam" in Joseph LaPalombara (ed), *Bureaucracy and Political Development* (Princeton: Princeton University Press).

Duby, Georges (1977) *The Chivalrous Society* (translated by Cynthia Postam) (Stanford, CA: Stanford University Press).

Eckstein, Harry (1982) "The Idea of Political Development: From Dignity to Efficiency" *World Politics* 34: 451-486.

Edwards, Carolyn (1975) "Societal Complexity and Moral Development: A Kenyan Study" *Ethos* 3:505-527.

Eisenstadt, S.N., and René Lemarchand (eds) (1981) *Political Clientalism, Patronage and Development* (Beverly Hills, CA: Sage).

Elder, Charles D., and Roger W. Cobb (1983) *The Political Uses of Symbols* (New York: Longman).

Fenno, Richard, Jr. (1978) *Home Style: House Members in Their Districts* (Boston: Little, Brown).

Fishkin, J. (1982) *Beyond Subjective Morality* (New Haven: Yale University Press).

Fitzgibbon, Russell (1956) "A Statistical Evaluation of Latin American Democracy" *Western Political Quarterly* 9(September):607-619.

Flavell, John H. (1963) *The Developmental Psychology of Jean Piaget* (New York: Van Nostrand).

——— (1968) *The Development of Role-Taking and Communication Skills in Children* (New York: Wiley).

Fowler, J.W. (1981) *Stages of Faith: The Psychology of Human Development and the Quest for Meaning* (San Francisco: Harper and Row).

Frey, Frederick (1971) "Developmental Aspects of Administration" in J. Paul Leagous and Charles P. Loomis (eds), *Behavioral Change in Administration* (Ithaca, NY: Cornell University Press), pp.219-272.

Gavaghan, Mary P., Kevin D. Arnold, and John C. Gibbs (1983) "Moral Judgment in Delinquents and Nondelinquents: Recognition versus Production Measures" *Journal of Psychology* 114:267-274.

Geertz, Clifford (1984) "Anti Anti-Relativism" *American Anthropologist* 86:263-278.

Gibbs, John (1977) "Kohlberg's Stages of Moral Judgment: A Constructive Critique" *Harvard Educational Review* 47:43-61.

Gilligan, Carol (1977) "In a Different Voice: Women's Conceptions of Self and Morality" *Harvard Educational Review* 47 (November):481-517.

——— (1982) *In a Different Voice: Psychological Theory and Women's Development* (Cambridge, MA: Harvard University Press).

Gilligan, Carol, Lawrence Kohlberg, Joan Lerner, and Mary Belenky (1971) "Moral Reasoning about Sexual Dilemmas." Technical Report of the Commission on Obscenity and Pornography, Vol. 1 (No. 52560010) (Washington, D.C.: U.S. Government Printing Office).

Gilligan, Carol, and J. M. Murphy (1979) "Development from Adolescence to Adulthood: The Philosopher and the 'Dilemma of the Fact'" in D. Kuhn (ed), *Intellectual Development Beyond Childhood* (San Francisco: Jossey-Bass).

Goulet, Denis (1968) "Development for What?" *Comparative Political*

Studies 1:295-312.

———(1971) *The Cruel Choice: A New Concept in the Theory of Development* (New York: Athenaeum).

Gramsci, Antonio (1957) *The Modern Prince and Other Writings* (trans. by Louis Marks) (New York: International Publishers).

Grew, Raymond (ed) (1978) *Crises of Political Development in Europe and the United States* (Princeton, NJ: Princeton University Press).

Habermas, Jürgen (1975) *Legitimation Crisis* (Boston: Beacon Press).

——— (1979) *Communication and the Evolution of Society* (Boston: Beacon Press).

——— (1979a) "What Is Universal Pragmatics?" in Habermas (1979:1-68).

——— (1979b) "Moral Development and Ego Identity" in Habermas (1979:69-94).

——— (1979c) "Historical Materialism and the Development of Normative Structures" in Habermas (1979:95-129)

——— (1979d) "Toward a Reconstruction of Historical Materialism" in Habermas (1979:130-177).

——— (1979e) "Legitimation Problems in the Modern State" in Habermas (1979:178-205).

——— (1982) "A Reply to My Critics" in John B. Thompson and David Held (eds), *Habermas: Critical Debates* (Cambridge, MA: MIT Press).

——— (1983) "Interpretive Social Science vs. Hermaneuticism" in Norma Haan, Robert N. Bellah, Paul Rabinow, and William M. Sullivan (eds), *Social Science as Moral Inquiry* (New York: Columbia University Press).

Hagen, Everett (1962) *On the Theory of Social Change: How Economic Growth Begins* (Homewood, IL: Dorsey Press).

Hall, Anthony (1977) "Patron-Client Relations: Concepts and Terms" in Schmidt et al. (eds), (1977:510-512).

Hallpike, C.R. (1979) *The Foundations of Primitive Thought* (New York: Oxford University Press).

Hennessy, Bernard (1985) *Public Opinion* (5th edition) (Monterey, CA: Brooks/Cole).

Hewitt, John (1979) *Self and Society: A Symbolic Interactionist Social Psychology* (2nd edition) (Boston: Allyn and Bacon).

Higgins, E. Tory, Diane Ruble, and Willard Hartup (eds) (1983) *Social Cognition and Social Development: A Sociocultural Perspective* (New York: Cambridge University Press).

Hobhouse, Lawrence Trelawney (1906) *Morals in Evolution* (London: Chapman and Hall). (A 1951, single-volume reprint of the 1906 edition).

Holt, Robert T., and John E. Turner (1975) "Crises and Sequences in Collective Theory Development" *American Political Science Review* 69:979-994.

Hope, Kempe Ronald (1985) "Electoral Politics and Political Development in Post-independence Guyana" *Electoral Studies* 4:57-68.

Huntington, Samuel P. (1965) *Political Order in Changing Societies* (New Haven: Yale University Press).

——— (1971) "The Change to Change: Modernization, Development, and Politics" *Comparative Politics* 3(3, April):283-322.

——— (1987) "The Goals of Development" in Weiner and Huntington (eds) (1987:3-32).

Jackins, Harvey (1987) "Understanding and Using Organizational Forms" in *The Longer View* (Seattle: Rational Island Publishers).

Jaguaribe, Helio (1973) *Political Development: A General Theory and A Latin American Case Study* (New York: Harper and Row).

Katz, Elihu (1957) "The Two-Step Flow of Communications: An Up-to-Date Report on the Hypothesis" *Public Opinion Quarterly* 21:61-78.

Katz, Elihu, and Paul Lazarsfeld (1955) *Personal Influence: The Part Played by People in the Flow of Mass Communications* (Glencoe, IL: Free Press).

Kemeny, Jim (1976) *An Interactionist Approach to Macro Sociology* (Gothenburg, Sweden: University of Gothenburg, Department of Sociology, Monograph 10).

Khalilzad, Zalmay (1984-5) "The Politics of Ethnicity in Southwest Asia: Political Development or Political Decay?" *Political Science Quarterly* 99(4, Winter):657-679.

Kingdon, John (1973) *Congressmen's Voting Decisions* (New York: Harper and Row).

Kohlberg, Lawrence (1981) *Essays on Moral Development: Vol. I. The Philosophy of Moral Development* (San Francisco: Harper and Row).

——— (1981a) "From Is to Ought: How to Commit the Naturalistic Fallacy and Get Away with It in the Study of Moral Development" in Kohlberg (1981:101-189).

——— (1981b) "Justice as Reversibility: The Claim to Moral Adequacy of a Highest Stage of Moral Judgment" in Kohlberg (1981:190-226).

——— (1981c) "Appendix. The Six Stages of Moral Judgment" in Kohlberg (1981:409-412).

——— (1984) *Essays on Moral Development: Vol. II. The Psychology of Moral Development* (San Francisco: Harper and Row).

——— (1984a) "Stage and Sequence: The Cognitive-Developmental Approach to Socialization" in Kohlberg (1984:7-169).

———(1984b) "Appendix A: The Six Stages of Justice Judgment" in Kohlberg (1984:621-639).

Kohlberg, Lawrence, and Daniel Candee (1984) "The Relationship of Moral Judgment to Moral Action" in Kurtines and Gewirtz (1984: Ch. 4).

Kohlberg, Lawrence, and R. Kramer (1969) "Continuities and Discontinuities in Childhood and Adult Moral Development" *Human Development* 12:93-120.

Kohlberg, Lawrence, Charles Levine, and Alexandra Hewer (1984a) "The Current Form of the Theory" in Kohlberg (1984:212-319).

Kohlberg, Lawrence, Charles Levine, and Alexandra Hewer (1984b) "Synopses and Detailed Replies to Critics" in Kohlberg (1984:320-386).

Kuhn, Deanna, Jonas Langer, Lawrence Kohlberg, and Norma Haan (1977) "The Development of Formal Operations in Logical and Moral Judgment" *Genetic Psychology Monographs* 95:97-188.

Kuhn, Thomas (1970a) *The Structure of Scientific Revolutions* (Chicago: University of Chicago Press).

——— (1970b) "Logic of Discovery or Psychology of Research?" and "Reflections on My Critics" in Imre Lakatos and Alan Musgrave (eds), *Criticism and the Growth of Knowledge* (New York: Cambridge University Press).

Kurtines, W., and J. Gewirtz (eds) (1984) *Morality, Moral Behavior and Moral Development* (New York: Wiley).

Lande, Carl H. (1977) "Group Politics and Dyadic Politics: Notes for a Theory" in Schmidt et al. (eds) (1977:506-510).

Levin, Alfred (1973) *The Third Duma: Election and Profile* (Hamden, CT: Archon Books).

Lewy, Guenter (1982) *False Consciousness: An Essay on Mystification* (New Brunswick, NJ: Transaction Books).

Lichter, L., and S. Lichter (1983) *Prime Time Crime: Criminals and Law Enforcers in TV Entertainment* (Washington, DC: The Media Institute).

Lieberman, Marcus (1972) "An Application of Samejima's Graded Scores Model: The Development of Moral Judgment" (Paper presented at the Spring 1972 Conference of the Psychometric Society, Princeton, NJ).

Loevinger, Jane (1966) "The Meaning and Measurement of Ego Development" *American Psychologist* 21:195-206.

Luckmann, Thomas (1963) *Das Problem der Religion in der modernen Gesellschaft* (Freiburg).

Lukács, Georg (1914) "Zur Soziologie des modernen Dramas" *Archiv für Sozialwissenschaften und Sozial Politik,* pp.303-345,662-706.

——— (1971) "Reification and the Consciousness of the Proletariat" in *History and Class Consciousness: Studies in Marxist Dialectics* (Cambridge, MA: MIT Press), pp.83-222.

Mansbridge, Jane J. (1986) *Why We Lost the ERA* (Chicago: University of Chicago Press).

Marcuse, Herbert (1965) "Repressive Tolerance" in Wolff, Robert Paul, Barrington Moore, Jr., and Herbert Marcuse, *A Critique of Pure Tolerance* (Boston: Beacon Press), pp.81-117.

Maslow, Abraham (1954) *Motivation and Personality* (New York: Harper and Brothers).

McCarthy, Thomas (1979) "Translator's Introduction" in Habermas (1979:vii-xxiv).

McClelland, David (1976) *The Achieving Society* (New York: Irvington).

McMillian, J., and S. Ragan (1983) "The Presidential Press Conference: A Study in Escalating Institutionalization" *Presidential Studies Quarterly* 12:231-241.

Medhurst, M. (1977) "American Cosmology and the Rhetoric of Inaugural Prayer" *Central States Speech Journal* 28:272-282.

Montes, Segundo (1979) *El Compadrazgo* (San Salvador: UCA Editors).

Monti, Joseph (1982) *Ethics and Public Policy: The Conditions of Public Moral Discourse* (Washington, DC: University Press of America).

Nisan, Mordecai, and Lawrence Kohlberg (1984) "Cultural Universality of Moral Judgment Stages: A Longitudinal Study in Turkey" in Kohlberg (1984:582-593).

Ono, Shin'ya (1965) "The Limits of Bourgeois Pluralism" *Studies on the Left* 5(Summer):46-72.

Overly, N. (ed) (1970) *The Unstudied Curriculum* (Washington, D.C.: Association for Supervision and Curriculum Development).

Overton, Willis F. (1983) *The Relationship between Social and Cognitive Development* (Hillsdale, NJ: Erlbaum).

Parenti, Michael (1978) *Power and the Powerless* (New York: St. Martin's).

——— (1983) *Democracy for the Few* (4th edition) (New York: St. Martin's).

Park, Han S. (1984) *Human Needs and Political Development* (Cambridge, MA: Schenkman).

Parsons, Talcott, and Edward Shils (eds) (1951) *Toward a General Theory of Action: Theoretical Foundations for the Social Sciences* (New York: Harper and Row).

Payne, James L. (1984) *Foundations of Empirical Political Analysis* (2nd printing) (College Station, TX: Lytton).

Perry, W.G., Jr. (1970) *Forms of Intellectual and Ethical Development in the College Years* (New York: Holt, Rinehart and Winston).

Piaget, Jean (1932) *The Moral Judgment of the Child* (London: Kegan Paul).

——— (1970) *Structuralism* (New York: Basic Books).

——— (1977) *Etudes Sociologique* (Geneva: Librairie Droz).

Pirenne, Henri (1952) *Medieval Cities: Their Origins and the Revival of Trade* (trans. by Frank D. Halsey) (Princeton, NJ: Princeton University Press).

Plascov, Avi (1982) *Security in the Persian Gulf: Vol. 3. Modernization, Political Development, and Stability* (Totowa, NJ:

Allanheld, Osmun).

Poggi, Gianfranco (1978) *The Development of the Modern State: A Sociological Introduction* (Stanford, CA: Stanford University Press).

Pye, Lucian (ed) (1963) *Communications and Political Development* (Princeton, NJ: Princeton University Press).

Pye, Lucian (1966) *Aspects of Political Development* (Boston: Little, Brown).

—— (1966a) "The Concept of Political Development" in Pye (1966:31-48).

—— (1966b) "Democracy and Political Development" in Pye (1966:71-88).

—— (1978) "Foreword" in Grew (1978:v-viii).

Radding, Charles (1978) "Evolution of Medieval Mentalities: A Cognitive-Structural Approach" *American Historical Review* 83(3):577-597.

—— (1979) "Superstition to Science: Nature, Fortune, and the Passing of the Medieval Ordeal" *American Historical Review* 84:945-969.

—— (1985) *A World Made by Men: Cognition and Society, 400-1200* (Chapel Hill, NC: University of North Carolina Press).

Radkey, Oliver Henry (1950) *The Election to the Russian Constituent Assembly of 1917* (Cambridge, MA: Harvard University Press).

Rawls, John (1971) *A Theory of Justice* (Cambridge, MA: Belknap).

Rest, James (1972) *Comprehension of Social Moral Concepts Test* (unpublished test, University of Minnesota).

—— (1973) "The Hierarchical Nature of Moral Judgment" *Journal of Personality* 41:86-109.

—— (1976) "New Approaches in the Assessment of Moral Judgment" in Thomas Lickona (ed), *Moral Development and Behavior: Theory, Research and Social Issues* (New York: Holt, Rinehart and Winston), pp.198-218.

Riggs, Fred W. (1981) "The Rise and Fall of 'Political Development'" in Samuel L. Long (ed), *The Handbook of Political Behavior, Volume 4* (New York: Plenum).

Robinson, John P. (1976) "Interpersonal Influence in Election Campaigns: Two Step-flow Hypotheses" *Public Opinion Quarterly* 40:304-319.

Rose, Phyllis (1983) *Parallel Lives* (New York: Knopf).

Rosenwasser, M. (1969) "Six Senate War Critics and Their Appeals for Gaining Audience Response" *Communications Quarterly* 17:43-50.

Sampson, Samuel F. (1978) *Crisis in a Cloister* (Norwood, NJ: Ablex).

Schelling, Thomas (1980) *The Strategy of Conflict* (Cambridge, MA: Harvard University Press, first printed in 1960).

Schmidt, Steffan W., James C. Scott, Carl Lande, and Laura Guasti (eds) (1977) *Friends, Followers, and Factions: A Reader in*

Political Clientelism (Berkeley: University of California Press).

Schumpeter, J. A. (1949) *The Theory of Economic Development* (Cambridge, MA: Harvard University Press).

Selman, Robert (1971) "The Relation of Role-Taking to the Development of Moral Judgment in Children" *Child Development* 42:79-91.

Selman, Robert, and William Damon (1975) "The Necessity (But Insufficiency) of Social Perspective Taking for Conceptions of Justice at Three Early Levels" in David DePalma and Jeanne Foley (eds), *Moral Development: Current Theory and Research* (Hillsdale, NJ: Lawrence Erlbaum Associates), pp.57-73.

Shorter, E., and C. Tilly (1974) *Strikes in France 1830-1968* (New York: Cambridge University Press).

Sinclair, K. (1982) "British Prestige Press Editorials on Readership During 1979 Campaign" *Journalism Quarterly* 59:230-234ff.

Smith, Arthur K., Jr. (1969) "Socio-Economic Development and Political Democracy: A Causal Analysis" *Midwest Journal of Political Science* 13(February):95-125.

Snarey, John, Joseph Reimer, and Lawrence Kohlberg (1984) "Cultural Universality of Moral Judgment Stages: A Longitudinal Study in Israel" in Kohlberg (1984:594-620).

Sophocles (1947) *The Theban Plays* (translated and introduced by E. F. Watling) (Baltimore, MD: Penguin).

Stokes, Gale (1974) "Cognition and the Function of Nationalism" *Journal of Interdisciplinary History* 4(4, Spring):525-542.

Sollie, Finn (1984) "Polar Politics: Old Games in New Territories or New Patterns in Political Development?" *International Journal* 39:695-720.

Stone, Clarence N. (1980) "Systemic Power in Community Decision Making: A Restatement of Stratification Theory" *American Political Science Review* 74(4, December):978-990.

———— (1982) "Social Stratification, Nondecision-Making, and the Study of Community Power" *American Politics Quarterly* 10:275-302.

Turiel, Elliot (1966) "An Experimental Test of the Sequentiality of Developmental Stages in the Child's Moral Judgment" *Journal of Personality and Social Psychology* 3:611-618.

———— (1974) "Conflict and Transition in Adolescent Moral Development" *Child Development* 45:14-29.

———— (1977) "Conflict and Transition in Adolescent Moral Development: II. The Resolution of Disequilibrium Through Structural Reorganization" *Child Development* 48:634-637.

Turiel, Elliot, Carolyn Pope Edwards, and Lawrence Kohlberg (1978) "Moral Development in Turkish Children, Adolescents, and Young Adults" *Journal of Cross-Cultural Psychology* 9(1):75-86.

Van Dijk, T. (1983) "Discourse Analysis: Its Development and

Application to the Structure of News" *Journal of Communication* 33:20-43.

Walker, Lawrence (1980) "Cognitive and Perspective-Taking Requirements for Moral Development" *Child Development* 51:131-139.

————— (1983) "Sources of Cognitive Conflict for Stage Transition in Moral Development" *Developmental Psychology* 19:103-110.

Watling, E.F. (1947) "Introduction" in Sophocles (1947), pp.7-22.

Weiner, Myron, and Samuel P. Huntington (eds) (1987) *Understanding Political Development* (Boston: Little, Brown).

Weinreich, Helen (1977) "Some Consequences of Replicating Kohlberg's Original Moral Development Study on a British Sample" *Journal of Moral Education* 7(1):32-39.

White, Harrison, Scott Boorman, and Ronald Breiger (1975) "Social Structure from Multiple Networks: I. Blockmodels of Roles and Positions" *American Journal of Sociology* 81(4):730-780.

White, Stephen (1977) "The USSR: Patterns of Autocracy and Industrialism" in Archie Brown and Jack Gray (eds), *Political Culture and Political Change in Communist States* (New York: Holmes and Meier).

Williamson, Judith (1978) *Decoding Advertisements* (London: Marion Boyars).

Wolfinger, Raymond E. (1971) "Nondecisions and the Study of Local Politics" and "Rejoinder to Frey's 'Comment'" *American Political Science Review* 65(4, December):1063-1080, 1102-1104.

Wolin, Sheldon (1960) *The Politics of Vision: Continuity and Innovation in Western Political Thought* (Boston: Little, Brown).

Wright, Thomas C. (1984) "The First Ibañez Administration in Chile (1927-1931): A Preliminary Assessment" (Paper presented at the Rocky Mountain Council on Latin American Studies Annual Meeting, Tucson, AZ, February 23-25).

Wynn, Thomas (1980) "The Intelligence of Later Acheulean Hominids" *Man* (N.S.) 14:371-391.

Yeager, F. (1974) "Linguistic Analysis of Oral Edited Discourse" *Communications Quarterly* 22:29-36.

Index

Absolutism, 68,72. *See also* Stage 4
Academic disciplines, division among, 3
Accommodation function, 41,42. *See also* Genetic epistemology
Acquiescence, 36
Action, 24
Adaptation function, 41,42. *See also* Genetic epistemology
Agape, 43,55,68. *See also* Stage 6
Antigone, 50,51,65
Aristotle, 79
Arnold, Kevin D., 59,116
Assimilation function, 41,42. *See also* Genetic epistemology
Auster, Richard D., 102,113

Bachrach, Peter, 91,113
Baratz, Morton, 91,113
Barter and trading, 43,46,65,68,70. *See also* Stage 2
Behaviorism, 24

Belenky, Mary, 116
Bellah, Robert N., 117
Benedict, Ruth, 43,113
Bensel, Richard F., 5,18,102,114
Bertilson, H., 40,114
Bianchi, Robert, 101,114
Binder, Leonard, 80,95,97,112,114
Bloch, Marc, 3,48,65,70,76,114
Blockmodeling, 30,31
Boorman, Scott, 30,31,123
Breiger, Ronald, 30,31,123
Bribery, 35,43,46,68,69,106. *See also* Stage 2
Bronfenbrenner, Urie, 100,114
Brown, Archie, 35,113,114,116,121, 123
Bullies, 44–46,69,76. *See also* Stage 1
Bureaucracy, 25,68, 72,88,106,115. *See also* Stage 4
Burg, Steven L., 111,114

Candee, Daniel, 21,57,118
Capacity, 105–107. *See also* Development syndrome
Capitalism, 68,73,77. *See also* Stage 5
Caporale, R., 115
Chapman, John W., 115,117
Chesler, Robert, 40,114
Chilcote, Ronald, 79,114
Chile, 77
Chilton, Stephen, 14,19,21,30,35,114
Chivalry, 48,71. *See also* Stage 3
Civil rights and liberties, 68,73,81. *See also* Stage 5
Clientelism, 68,70,71,121. *See also* Exchange patronage; Social patronage; Stage 2; Stage 3
Cobb, Roger W., 4,20,116
Cognition, 60,61,63,66,117,121, 122
Cognitive ambiguity, 2,3

Cognitive development, 3,14,42,67,104,110; horizontal decalage in, 61,62,66; related to moral development, 60,61; synchrony and asynchrony, 61. *See also* Moral development

Cognitive dynamics, 36,38,58–62,66,80–88,99. *See also* Moral development

Cognitive structure(s), 2,38,61,67,104

Cognitive structures, 102

Colby, Ann, 14,38,49,59,62–64, 114

Coleman, James S., 112,113

Committee on Comparative Politics (SSRC/CCP), 102,105–107,112

Communication and communication networks, 20,25,38,40,43,55, 68,83–85,89,93,96,97, 103

Compadrazgo, 43,48,65,68,120. *See also* Stage 3

Composition fallacy, 86

Congress, 30

Constitutional democracy, 1,2,7,68,73. *See also* Stage 5

Conventional level of moral reasoning, 47. *See also* Stage 3; Stage 4

Corporatism, 68. *See also* Stage 3

Corvee labor, 43,46,65,68. *See also* Stage 2

Courtly love, 43,48,68. *See also* Stage 3

Creationism, 81,82,99. *See also* Stage 4

Crenson, Matthew, 91,115

Cultural breakdown, 26,27

Cultural innovation, 92,93

Cultural relativism, ethnocentrism, and universality, 1,2,13,38,43,52,63, 64,74,75,76,85,102, 104,106,107,110–112,116

Cultural reasoning, 40,41

Cultural system, 3,16,18,26–33. *See also* Individual system; Political culture; Political development

Curses, 43,46,68. *See also* Stage 2

Danet, Brenda, 25,88,115

Davies, James Chowning, 66,115

Decalage, 61,62,66,93,104

Defining Issues Test, 59

Deontological moralities, 56,62

DePalma, David, 122

Dependency theory, 111

Deterrence, 43,46

Deutsch,Karl W., 8,77, 115

Development, 1–21,23,27–29,33–35, 37,39,42,44,48,56, 58–63,65–67,69,74–77,79–82,84–86,88, 93–107,109–123. *See also* Moral development; Political development

Development syndrome, capacity, 105–107; differentiation, 105,106,112; equality, 105. *See also* Political development

Developmental dynamics, 17,18,33,34,79–100. *See also* Moral development; Political development

DeVries, Rheta, 61,115

Differentiation, 105,106,112. *See also* Development syndrome

Döbert, Rainer, 15,17,99

Dobelstein, Andrew W., 18,115

Dog, wagged by tail, 110

Domination, 43,44,68. *See also* Stage 1

Dominguez, Jorge I., 77,115

Dorsey, John T., Jr., 8,115,117

Dualism, 68,71. *See also* Stage 3

Duby, Georges, 71,97,115

Due process, 68,73. *See also* Stage 5

Eckstein, Harry, 5,66,115

Economic development, 5. *See also* Political development

Economic institutions, 4. *See also* Politics, definition of

Edwards, Carolyn Pope, 38,49,115,122

Efficacy, 7. *See also* Development syndrome

Eichmann, Adolph, 64
Eisenstadt, S. N.,
    70,116
Elder, Charles D.,
    4,20,116
Empathy, 7
Equal Rights
    Amendment
    (ERA), 119
Equality, 105. *See also*
    Development
    syndrome
Estates. *See Staende*
Ethnocentrism. *See*
    Cultural
    relativism,
    ethnocentrism, and
    universality
Exact specification,
    challenge of,
    6–9,19,34–35. *See
    also* Five
    fundamental
    theoretical
    challenges facing
    political
    development
    conceptions
Exchange, 70. *See also*
    Stage 2
Exchange patronage,
    68,70,71. *See also*
    Clientelism; Social
    patronage; Stage 2
Extortion, 43,68,69,76.
    See also Stage 1

Fair competition,
    43,68,73,74. *See
    also* Stage 2
False consciousness,
    91,92
Fascism, 68,72. *See
    also* Stage 4
Fenno, Richard, Jr.,
    30,116
Feudal fealty,
    43,46,48,68. *See
    also* Stage 2; Stage
    3
Feudalism, early and
    late, 68,70,76. *See*

also Stage 2; Stage
    3
Feuds, 47,48,70. *See
    also* Stage 2
Fierke, K., 40,114
Fishkin, James, 63,116
Fitzgibbon, Russell,
    7,116
Five fundamental
    theoretical
    challenges facing
    political
    development
    conceptions,
    1–21,35,79,87,88,99,
    101; as guides to
    fruitful research,
    14,16. *See also
    specific challenges*
Flavell, John H.,
    61,63,64,116
Foley, Jeanne, 122
Forces of production,
    103
Foreign policy and
    international
    relations,
    4,109–111
Fowler, J. W., 62,116
Frey, Frederick,
    69,99,116,123
Friendship, 43,47,48.
    See also Stage 3

Gavaghan, Mary P.,
    59,116
Geertz, Clifford,
    63,64,116
Genetic epistemology,
    2,4,15–17,60,74–76,
    99,103. *See also*
    Piaget, Jean
Gewirtz, J., 118,119
Gibbs, John C.,
    59,63,114,116
Gilligan, Carol,
    49,61,63,65,66,75,
    116
Golden Rule, concrete,
    43,47,48; second-
    order, 43,55. *See
    also* Stage 3; Stage 6

Goulet, Denis, 8,19,116
Governmental
    institutions. See
    Politics, definition
    of
Gramsci, Antonio,
    112,117
Gray, Jack, 114,123
Grew, Raymond,
    95–97,109,112,117,
    121
Guasti, Laura, 121

Haan, Norma, 117,119
Habermas, Jürgen,
    13,15,20,21,26,36,37,
    55,56,62,63,65,81,90,
    94,95,99,103,117,
    119
Hagen, Everett,
    7,9,28,117
Hall, Anthony, 71,117
Hallpike, C. R.,
    15,17,117
"Hard structural" vs.
    "soft structural"
    stage theories,
    62,66
Harre, R., 115
Hartshorne, H., 66
Hartup, Willard,
    63,66,117
Heclo, Hugh, 77,115
Hegel, 102,103,107
Hegemonic power,
    3,14,29,33,90–92,95,
    96,98–100,103,104,
    110. *See also*
    Public
    commonness
Held, David, 29,117
Hennessy, Bernard,
    99,117
Hermann, Margaret B.,
    115
Hewer, Alexandra,
    38,56,62–66,119
Hewitt, John, 29,117
Hidden curriculum,
    31,32,36,91. *See
    also* Hegemonic
    power

Higgins, E. Tory,
  63,66,117
History,
  4,12,18,32,34,36,79,
  87,90,95–97,100,102,
  104. *See also*
  Public
  commonness
Hobbes, Thomas, 19, 77
Hobhouse, Lawrence
  Trelawney,
  15,17,18,21,76,79,
  98,104,117
Holt, Robert T.,
  112,117,120,121
Hope, Kempe Ronald,
  18,19,117
Hostages, 68,69. *See
  also* Stage 2
Human nature,
  concepts of in
  original position,
  112; concepts of in
  social science,
  107,108; Marxian
  concept of, 112
Huntington, Samuel P.,
  5–8,11,18,19,102,
  118,123

Ibañez administration
  (Chile), 77
Idealism,
  12,47–49,55,59,67,
  72,80,102,103
Idealistic fallacy, 12
Ideological thought,
  91,92
Individual beliefs, 29
Individual evaluations
  of ways of relating,
  29,30. *See also*
  Public
  commonness
Individual rights,
  43,53. *See also*
  Stage 5
Individual system,
  3,16,26–29,31–33.
  See also Cultural
  system; Social
  system

Inertia, 89,90,98
Institutions, social and
  political,
  2–4,7,9,10,23,30,31,
  34,36,67–75,80,85,
  86,92,102,110. *See
  also* Social system;
  Cultural system
Instrumental purpose
  and exchange,
  43,45. *See also*
  Stage 2
Integration,
  differentiation, and
  coordination of
  cognitive
  structures and/or
  moral perspectives,
  24,35,38,42,45,50,51,
  53,55,56,102,105–
  107,112. *See also*
  Moral
  development,
  dynamics of
Intentionality, 24,35
Interpersonal relations.
  See Ways of
  relating
Inversions, 85,86,99

Jackins, Harvey, 74,118
Jaguaribe, Helio,
  111,118
Jefferson, Thomas, 73
Jensen, U. J., 115
Justice,
  15,42,54,55,84,85,
  87,109,110,112,114,
  118,121,122

Kant, Immanuel, 56
Katz, L., 83,115,118
Kemeny, Jim, 29,118
Khalilzad, Zalmay,
  18,101,118
Kingdon, John, 30,118
Kohlberg, Lawrence,
  2,14,17,20,21,36,38–
  44,46,47,49,50,52–
  66,74,75,88,104,
  107,114–116,118–
  120,122,123

Kramer, R., 66,118
Kuhn, Deanna,
  17,61,77,116,119
Kurtines, William,
  118,119

Lakatos, Imre, 119
Lande, Carl H.,
  70,119,121
Langer, Jonas, 119
LaPalombara, Joseph,
  115
Law and order, 43. *See
  also* Stage 4
Lazarsfeld, Paul,
  83,118
Leagous, J. Paul, 116
Legitimacy,
  13,32,84–86
Lemarchand, René,
  70,116
Lerner, Joan, 116
Levin, Alfred, 20,119
Levine, Charles,
  38,56,62–66,119
Lewy, Guenter, 92,119
Lichter, S., 40,119
Lickona, Thomas, 121
Lieberman, Marcus,
  61,114,119
Locke, John, 73
Locus of development,
  challenge of
  specifying,
  6,19,20,23–29,96.
  See also Five
  fundamental
  theoretical
  challenges facing
  political
  development
  conceptions
Loevinger, Jane, 62,119
Long, Samuel L., 121
Loomis, Charles P., 116
Lord of the Flies, 76
Luckmann, Thomas,
  99,119
Lukács, Georg,
  3,90,111,113,119
Lying, 45

Mansbridge, Jane J., 87,119
Marcuse, Herbert, 85,119
Marx, Karl, and Marxism, 4,12,79,102–104,107, 111,112; "vulgar Marxism," 103,104
Maslow, Abraham, 10,28,62,119
May, M. A., 66
McCarthy, Thomas, 63,119
McClelland, David, 7,28,36,40,64,120
McMillian, J., 40,120
Medhurst, M., 40,120
Medieval cities, 68,71,72,92,93. *See also* Stage 3
Micro-macro connection, challenge of specifying, 1,2,4,6,9,10,16,20, 29–34,99. *See also* Five fundamental theoretical challenges facing political development conceptions
Military, 68,72
Modernity and progress theorists, 11,13
Montes, Segundo, 65,120
Monti, Joseph, 37,120
Moore, Barrington, Jr., 119
Moral development, 17,38,42,56,58,67; affected by political culture, 59; and moral behavior, 37,57,63,66; "awareness" milepost, 59,60,82,83; dynamics of, 58–62,80,86,110;

horizontal decalage in, 61,62,66,93,94,96, 100,104;"ignorance" milepost, 59; inevitability of, 58,86; measurement of, 39–41,63,64,66,75; "preference" milepost, 59,60,64,82,83,104; "reproduction" milepost, 60,64,82; stage skipping in, 97; "teaching" milepost, 60; vertical decalage in, 49. *See also* Cognitive development; Stage 1; Stage 2; Stage 3; Stage 4; Stage 4 1/2; Stage 5; Stage 6
Moral reasoning, 2,3,37,56,58,63,67, 102,105,110; incomprehension of, 82–85
Moral stage problems and ambiguities, 43–46,48–52,54,57, 65,75,76,80–82,99, 102–104,110
Moral stages, advances in social average of, 86; declines in social average of, 86; social average of, 86
Murphy, J. M., 66,116
Musgrave, Alan, 119
Mutual care, 43,54,55,65,68. *See also* Stage 6
Mutual interpersonal expectations, 43,47. *See also* Public commonness
Mutual respect,

26,43,68,73,74. *See also* Stage 5
Mutual support of moral system, 43,50,51,68,72. *See also* Stage 4

Nature of development, challenge of specifying, 10,11,14,20,67–77. *See also* Five fundamental theoretical challenges facing political development conceptions
Nazism, 69
Need for achievement (*n* Ach), 7,36
Negative exchange, 69. *See also* Stage 2
Newtonian physics, 20,21
Nisan, Mordecai, 38,120
Nondecision-making, 91. *See also* Hegemonic forces
"Normal science", 43,68,74,77. *See also* Stage 5
Normative grounding, challenge of providing, 1,2,4–6,9,11–14,16, 20,34,35,37–66,85, 95,99,100,102,104– 106,108,109. *See also* Five fundamental theoretical challenges facing political development conceptions

Objectivating attitude, 13,20,26,27,33
Ono, Shin'ya, 100,120
Open question, 12,13

Original Position,
15,55,65,100
Overly, N., 36,91,120
Overton, Willis F.,
63,66,120

Parenti, Michael,
91,120
Park, Han S.,
20,66,111,120
Parsons, Talcott,
2,4,24–26,105,120
Payne, James L.,
10,19,120
Pecking order, 68,69.
See also Stage 1
Pennock, Roland, 115
Performative attitude,
13,20,26
Perry, W. G., Jr.,
62,120
Physical compulsion,
43,44,68. See also
Stage 1
Piaget, Jean,
4,10,15,21,24,39–
41,49,60,61,63,83,
87,115,116,120
Pirenne, Henri, 71,120
Plascov, Avi, 102,120
Poggi, Gianfranco,
46,71,72,76,120
Political culture,
2,14,23,31,34,58,
67,106,108,109;
availability and
visibility of
alternatives,
89–91; confusion in
definition of, 23;
cultural ignorance,
69; defined as all
public ways of
relating, 25;
dissent, 69;
measurement of,
40,41; "parochial,"
106; subcultures,
26,69,86,92–94,96;
unity of, 104. See
also Public
commonness; Ways

of relating
Political development,
complexity of
dynamics of,
97–99; confusion in
definition of,
5,6,18,19,101,111;
continuity of,
80,96,97; crises in,
80,96–98; cycles in,
79,95,96; defined
as a syndrome,
7,105; defined as
aggregated
changes of
individuals,
7,9,10,20,27,28,58;
defined as changes
in institutions,
9,10,18; defined as
economic growth,
5,101; defined as
institutional
changes, 7; defined
as political
change,
5,6,11–13,101,102;
defined as
modernization,
101; defined as
structural stage
development of
political culture,
14,28,43,58,68;
defined as
syndrome,
105–107,112;
defined as
Westernization,
101; dynamics of,
2,14,58,69,86,110;
horizontal decalage
in, 93,94,96;
horizontal decalage
of, 104; human
agency in, 95;
importance of, 4;
inevitability of,
79,86,94–96,98,104;
monotonicity of,
79,95; regression
and retrogression

in, 95,96,98; stage
skipping in, 96–98;
synchrony and
asynchrony of,
79,80,96,98;
unilinearity of,
74–76,79,80,94,110.
See also
Development;
Development
syndrome; Moral
development
Political economy, 3
Political institutions, 4
Politics, definition of,
3,34,35
Polybius, 79
Positive exchange, 69.
See also Stage 2
Postconventional and
principled level of
moral reasoning,
52. See also Stage
5; Stage 6
Power of ideas, 12,14.
See also
Hegemonic power
Pre-literate societies,
64
Prebend, 43,46,65,68.
See also Stage 2
Preconventional level of
moral reasoning,
44. See also Stage
1; Stage 2
Prescriptivity,
15,16,21,56–58,66
Prior rights and social
contract, 43. See
also Stage 5
Prisons, 68,69,76
Public commonness,
3,14,17,18,25,26,
29–32,35,58,67,80,
89–92,103,104,106,
110; dynamics of,
80
Punishment and
obedience, 43,44.
See also Stage 1
Pye, Lucian,
2,7,79,95,99,101,

105,106,111,112,
121

Rabinow, Paul, 117
Radding, Charles,
15,17,18,40,64,69,
71,87,121
Radkey, Oliver Henry,
20,121
Ragan, S., 40,120
Rational debate,
43,54,68,73. *See
also* Stage 5
Rawls, John,
15,18,55,56,65,71,
74,76,85,100,112,
121
Reasoning, 3,7
Reasoning structures,
24,25
Reflective equilibrium,
18.
Regression and
retrogression. See
Moral
development;
Political
development
Regular patterns of
interaction,
26,27,30–33. *See
also* Social system
Reimer, Joseph, 38,122
Relations of production,
103,104
Religion,
3,34,51,72,81,99,
102
Replication of
relationships,
67–70,76,77
Repression, 85,86. *See
also* Hegemonic
power
Rest, James,
54,59,60,64,66,75,
121
Retrogression of moral
or cultural stages,
38,56,58,65,66,95
Revenge,
43,45–48,54,68–70.

See also Stage 2
Revolutionary or
deviant
subcultures, 26.
See also Political
culture
Riggs, Fred W.,
5,111,121
Rightness, 26,37,38.
See also Validity
claims
Robinson, John P.,
99,121
Role-taking and social
cognition, 61,66
Romantic love,
43,48,68. *See also*
Stage 3
Rose, Phyllis, 64,121
Rosenwasser, M.,
40,121
Ruble, Diane, 63,66,117
Rule, 71,72. *See also*
Stage 3; Stage 4

Sampson, Samuel F.,
30,121
Satyagraha, 43,55,68.
See also Stage 6
Schelling, Thomas,
88,89,121
Schmidt, Steffan W.,
70,117,119,121
Schumpeter, J. A.,
28,121
Science, 68,77. *See
also* "Normal
science"; Stage 5
Scott, James C.,
121,123
Seizure by force, 43,68.
See also Stage 1
Selman, Robert,
60,61,63,64,122
Shils, Edward, 25,120
Shorter, E., 40,122
Silver, Morris, 102,113
Sinclair, K., 40,122
Slavery, 68,69,76. *See
also* Stage 1
Smith, Adam, 73
Smith, Arthur K., Jr.,

7,122
Snarey, John, 38,122
Social contract, 52,53.
See also Stage 5
Social Darwinism,
17,98
Social development.
See Political
development
Social inertia, 14
Social institutions. *See*
Politics, definition
of
Social patronage,
48,68,71. *See also*
Clientelism;
Exchange
patronage; Stage 3
Social science, 107,108;
laws of, 108
Social Science Research
Council (SSRC),
102,105–107,112.
See also
Committee on
Comparative
Politics
Social structure, 31
Social system,
3,16,26–33,35;
maintenance of,
43. *See also*
Cultural system;
Individual system;
Regular patterns of
interaction
Socialization,
29,31,32,91,100
Sollie, Finn, 18,122
Sophocles,
50,51,122,123
Spengler, Oswald, 79
Springer, D., 40,114
Stability, 84,86
Staende, 68,71,72. *See
also* Stage 3
Staendestaat, 68,71.
See also Stage 3
Stage 1,
42–45,49,51,59,63–
65,68,69,76
Stage 2,

43,45–50,53,54,59, 65,68,69,71,74–76

Stage 3, 43,47–51,55–57,59, 64,65,68,70–73,81, 107

Stage 4, 43,49,50–53,56,57, 59,65,68,72,73,81, 82,84,99,107

Stage 4½, 52,53,63

Stage 5, 43,49,52–57,68,73, 74,81,82,107

Stage 6, 42,43,49,54–56,63– 65,68

Stage skipping, 38,56,58. See also Moral development; Political development

Stages of cultural reasoning. See Political development

Stages of moral reasoning, 38,42–56,63,68,82. See also specific stages

Steady-state society, 31–33

Stokes, Gale, 15,17,122

Stone, Clarence N., 91,100,122

Structure-content distinction, 38,39,43,61,64,74, 75,80,104,105. See also Genetic epistemology

Sullivan, William M., 117

Support, 36

Survey research, 40

Symbolic interactionism, 2,16,23,29

Tail, wagging the dog, 110

Taiwan, 75

Tax farming, 68,69. See also Stage 2

Teleological moralities, 62

Theoretical agreement, achieved by analysis, 19,20; achieved by consensus, 19; achieved by fiat, 19

Theoretical levels of fields of intellectual inquiry, 15–18

Thompson, John B., 117

Threats, 43,44,68. See also Stage 1

Tilly, Charles, 40,122

Transitional level of moral reasoning. See Stage 4½

Truth, 26. See also Validity claims

Truthfulness, 26. See also Validity claims

Turiel, Elliot, 38,64,81,122

Turkey, 114,120

Turner, John E., 112,117

Two-step flow of communications, 83,84

Tyranny of majority rule, 68,72. See also Stage 4

Undistorted communicative action, 43,68

United States, 1,9,59,73,81,85,91, 92,100,108,111; as developing society, 108,109; political culture of, 100

Universal ethical principles, 43,54,55

Universality and universalizability of moral reasoning, 16,21,56,57,65,104, 105,110. See also Cultural relativism, ethnocentrism, and universality

Utility and utilitarianism, 43,52,53,71,107

Validity claims, 21,26,37,38. See also Habermas, Jürgen; Rightness; Truth; Truthfulness

Value dissensus, 27. See also Political culture

Vassalage, 43,46,68,71. See also Stage 2

Veil of Ignorance, 15,112

Vendettas, 70,76. See also Stage 2

Verba, Sidney, 7,28,54,72,113

Vietnam, 1,9

Walker, Lawrence, 62,81,122

Watling, E. F., 51,122,123

Ways of relating, 3,14,23–32,37–39, 43,44,58,63,67,80, 89,100,108,110. See also Political culture

Weiner, Myron, 5,118,123

Weinreich, Helen, 38,123

Western society, 13,14,20. See also United States

White, Harrison, 20,30,31,123

Williamson, Judith,

40,123
Withdrawal of status
    respect, 9
Wolff, Robert Paul, 119
Wolfinger, Raymond E.,
    91,100,123
Wolin, Sheldon,
    19,77,123
Wright, Thomas C.,
    77,123
Wynn, Thomas,
    15,17,123

Yeager, F., 40,123

About the Book and the Author

Professor Chilton defines political development by combining a Piagetian theory of the development of moral reasoning with a symbolic interactionist conception of political culture. Thus, he posits that political development is a (Piagetian) cognitive-developmental change in the political culture, both affecting and affected by political institutions and political actors. The specifics of each culture's tradition augment the universal developmental order of cognitive structures to create culturally specific developmental sequences. Developmental dynamics arise from the peculiarities of cognitive development and from the problems of establishing any new way people relate to one another.

The application of Piagetian psychology to symbolic interactionism, concludes Chilton, overcomes the two major problems that have plagued earlier definitions of political development: (1) connecting individual and institutional change in the development process (the micro-macro problem); and (2) defining development so that "more developed" is, in a cross-culturally valid sense, ethically "better" (the normative grounding problem).

Stephen Chilton is assistant professor of political science at the University of Minnesota at Duluth, where he specializes in conceptual analysis in the fields of comparative politics and political psychology.

135